MATCHMAKER SECRETS

The Six Predictors
of Dating Success

Elizabeth Cobey-Piper
and Susie Hardesty

Matchmaker Secrets, The Six Predictors of Dating Success

This publication is designed to provide accurate and authoritative information with regard to the subject matter covered. Although every precaution has been taken to verify the accuracy of the information contained herein, the authors and publisher assume no responsibility for any errors or omissions. No liability is assumed for damages that may result from the use of information contained within. The opinions expressed by the authors in this book are not endorsed by Best Seller Publishing® and are the sole responsibility of the authors rendering the opinion.

Books may be purchased by contacting the authors at: Matchmaker Secrets 20 North Street, Dublin, OH 43017 or call 1(614) 766-3283 or email at info@matchmakersecrets.com. Visit us online at www.MatchmakerSecrets.com

Published by: Best Seller Publishing® LLC, Pasadena, California

Cover Design by: John G. Piper, Piper Art Design

Editor: Luisa Canneto

Photography by: Terra Luna, Images by Terra Luna

Creative Consultant: Michol Childress

ISBN: 978-1517247348

1. Self Help 2. Dating 3. Relationships 4. Love

First Edition

Printed in The United States of America

We lovingly dedicate this book to...

All of the wonderful singles who are seeking love.

Our clients who have given us the honor of guiding them as they search for love, thank you for inviting us to join you on your amazing journeys.

Elizabeth:

For my husband, John G. Piper, whose love and support has given me joy and strength since the day we fell in love.

For my parents, Runa Brynjolfsdottir Cobey and Herbert T. Cobey, who taught me how to love and encouraged me to approach the world with curiosity and enthusiasm.

And for my sister, Alexandra B. Ford, whose lifetime of friendship and love have been an anchor in my life.

Susie:

For my parents, Wilford W. and Florentine E. Hardesty, who always chose love.

For my siblings, Von Hardesty and Diane Bailey Tupps, who encouraged me to tell our stories and always listened with avid interest.

And for my sisters, Judy Hardesty and Patricia Hardesty, who have ever been my loving advocates.

CONTENTS

ACKNOWLEDGMENTS

We would especially like to thank Luisa Canneto, our editor, for
her unwavering belief and dedication to this book
and its message.

We would also like to express our gratitude to the many
wonderful people who have given their time and support to help
us bring this book into the world: Michol Childress,
Linda Apple, Judy Hardesty, John Piper, Patricia Hardesty,
Von Hardesty, Alexandra Ford, John Karapelou,
Damon Bingman, Daniel Szabo, Sabrina Smith, Carol Fahmy,
Deborah Wasserman, Kristin Henkaline, Hilary St. Pierre,
René Lewis, Debbie Peterseim, and Leeanne Hester.

Predictors QUIZ

Do you want to know your odds of
dating success?

Before you read this book, take
the Six Predictors quiz and find out.

http://MatchmakerSecrets.com/quiz

After you've learned our secrets, take the quiz again
and see how your odds have improved!

You can search throughout the entire universe for someone who is more deserving of your love and affection than you are yourself, and that person is not to be found anywhere. You yourself, as much as anybody in the entire universe deserve your love and affection.

–Buddha

INTRODUCTION

INTRODUCTION

HOW MANY times have you been asked, "Why are you still single?"

How often have you heard people say, "How could someone so pretty, or handsome, or successful, or kind, or such an all-around great person, still be single?"

Inevitably, these questions boil down to one overriding judgment: what's wrong with you that you are still single?

The fundamental and prevailing misconception is this: if you have the outward signs of success, if you are attractive, confident, smart, funny, or a good person, and still can't find love, then there must be something wrong with you.

As professional matchmakers, our answer to this is simple—*there is nothing wrong with you at all!*

It isn't looks, money, age, or lack of baggage that will ensure you find love. Those things are part of the equation, but they are *not* the determining factors for dating success.

Along with this misconception, there are two other common fallacies about why people fail to find love. The first is market scarcity, meaning that there are not enough fish in the dating pool. However, according to the 2011 United States Census, there are over 100 million single adults in the United States. Surely, with such a heavily stocked pool, there are enough available people to meet.

The second fallacy that many singles believe is that they just haven't encountered the right candidates. They are confident that the only thing they need is to have quality matches put in front of them. Yet, in spite of having a long line of potential Mr. or Ms. Rights paraded before them as they endlessly date, love continues to elude them.

So, if there is nothing wrong with you, and there are millions of single people— even great candidates available, then what is the answer to the question, "Why are you still single?" And more importantly, how can you find love?

As two matchmakers who own a highly personalized matchmaking company, we consider these questions every day. We are part of a nationwide network of Certified Professional Matchmakers, who work with tens of thousands of singles who have been interviewed, screened, and approved as great candidates. As a result, we are certain that the problem is not a shortage of wonderful people.

We believe there is someone for everyone, and we are committed to each and every person we work with finding love.

It's a bold statement, and we stand by it and for it. That said, we live in the real world, and the inescapable fact is that not all of our clients find love. We have an excellent success rate, and seeing our clients find love is our greatest joy. When our clients aren't successful, that's just as important to us. It would be easy to ignore the failures, sweep them under the rug, leave them behind, and move on. But that's not how we operate. We *always* want to know why. As we follow our clients' progress and struggles, we ask ourselves, "What works, and what doesn't work? Why did she find love and why didn't he?"

Always asking "why" allowed us to identify the patterns of those who were successful and those who were not. This is how we discovered the *truth* about what predicts dating success.

The Epiphany:

We realized that how a person approaches their search for love is far more important than what they look like, what they have, or what they do for a living.

As matchmakers, we have worked closely with thousands of single men and women, carefully observing who was successful and who was not. We have distilled our observations into a concise set of factors. We call these factors **The Six Predictors of Dating Success**. These Predictors are the formula for how to approach dating so that you can be successful. When you implement them, you can fully enjoy the dating process and significantly increase your odds of finding love.

Once we identified these Six Predictors, we went back through our case files and found that our successful clients were effectively utilizing all six in their search for love. We also determined that the clients who failed to find love were missing at least one Predictor— in most cases, more than one. It very quickly became apparent to us that having just one or some of the Predictors wasn't enough. In order to succeed, in order to find love, all Six Predictors have to be in place. In just one meeting with a client, we can use the Predictors to project their likelihood of getting into a relationship. We help our clients understand which Predictors they need to develop and show them how the six work in unison, each supporting the others. When they utilize all Six Predictors, our clients become empowered, and the dating world becomes ripe with opportunity. The best news of all: **You have control over these Predictors.**

Once you know and understand The Six Predictors, you can change your approach to dating and your odds of finding love will greatly improve. Contrary to most conventional wisdom, *you* have a great deal of influence over your love life. You have the power to be successful, and we want to help you discover that power within yourself!

We will go through the Six Predictors one by one. We will share real life examples of both failure and success within each Predictor. What's more, we will offer our matchmaking insights and conclusions. We will share the secrets that took us over thirty years of combined experience to discover.

You will discover:

Why you haven't been successful in the past.

Where you need to focus and shift your attention.

How to turn the odds in your favor.

How to enjoy the dating process.

How to find love.

Most importantly, we will show you that you truly do have the power to be successful in love. We'd like to repeat that last

point, as it is an essential part of the process. **You have the power
to be successful!**

TWO MATCHMAKERS + ONE CONCLUSION = SIX PREDICTORS

Two Matchmakers + One
Conclusion = Six Predictors

WHEN WE began our matchmaking careers, both of us had the same preconceived notions about what made people easy or difficult to match. We believed that being beautiful, successful and baggage-free were the keys to finding love. The odds are that, like most people, you probably hold ideas that are similar to the assumptions we made in our early matchmaking days. As it turned out, we had a lot to learn.

The stories we share throughout this book are based on real experiences, however, in the interest of privacy, all of the names of the people we work with and some of the details have been changed. In a few cases, the characters are composites of several people with similar experiences.

Susie

When I started as a new matchmaker, I had very little guidance. My boss taught me the agency's policies and procedures, but when it came to learning the art and science of matchmaking, I was on my own. As far as guessing who was most matchable, I believed all the myths I had absorbed since childhood and what I'd learned from years of reading *Cosmopolitan* magazine.

Like my clients, I was looking for perfection and judged everyone based on superficial qualities. I didn't know how to investigate further. Learning to get beneath the surface would take years of practice— years of watching and listening to my clients. I believed, as do most, that the prettiest, most successful single person would be my ace, an effortless match. But, my thinking was turned on its head. I discovered that I was wrong about what predicted people's likelihood of finding love.

I'll always remember the client who gave me my first indication that popular culture doesn't have all the answers. Andrea was a middle-aged administrative assistant. She had a nice sense of style, but she was overweight and not particularly attractive. The thing that alarmed me the most about her appearance was her noticeably thinning hair. On the other hand, what I loved about her was her warm personality and her voice. It was the prettiest voice I had ever heard. I must admit, the more I listened to her story, the more I liked her. All the same, I was worried about her chances of attracting a man. I couldn't sleep that night, thinking about Andrea's odds of finding love and wondering if I had done her a disservice by taking her on as a client. But who was I to judge this woman?

I kept a careful eye on Andrea's progress and, before I knew it, she was engaged to a wonderful man. He was a nice-looking and successful architect, and he had delightful children who really cared about Andrea. Never having had children of her own, this was more than she could have imagined.

Watching Andrea find success really challenged my preconceptions. How could she have made it happen so fast?

Something was going on!

Elizabeth

When I was a new matchmaker, I remember having two exceptionally attractive clients sign with me in one week. Thinking that these women were going to be the easiest clients I could have ever asked for, I felt a little guilty for taking their money. The first was Emily. She was 39, an adorable, slim, blue-eyed blonde who looked a lot like Jennifer Aniston. The other was Hannah. She was 36, had long, dark, wavy hair, and stunning crystal blue eyes that could capture any man's heart. They were both smart and well-educated, with great jobs, and little or no "baggage." I thought that I'd gotten two of the world's easiest people to match. I just knew they would be in and out.

I matched each of them with one eligible bachelor after another. As I worked with Emily, I quickly realized that she was very picky. It wasn't only that she wanted someone tall, dark, and handsome, she also made it clear that gray hair, even a little at the temple, was a turn-off. Bald men and men with thinning hair were also out. Now, keep in mind that her natural dating pool was primarily men aged forty and over. Still, I managed to find several men who were her type, but she always found something about them that "just wasn't quite right." This went on for months. Eventually, I introduced her to Matthew, and he fit the bill. Finally, she liked someone! I was thrilled. Six months later I got a call from Matthew. He told me they'd had their first argument, and she had sent him packing. She'd told him that he "just wasn't quite right," for her.

Like Emily, Hannah struggled to find love. It wasn't that she was overly picky about who she would meet; instead, her obstacle was her expectation of *how* she would fall in love. Hannah was an introvert who took a long time to open up with new people. Still, she longed for an exciting connection with strong chemistry, and she expected it to be immediate. I introduced her to several men whom I knew she would like. Most of them found her attractive, but their feedback was always the same: Hannah was quiet, she didn't seem interested, or they just didn't "click." Even when the men were open to a second date with her, Hannah consistently turned them down. It was as though she was waiting for lightning to strike. After working with her for several months, I came to realize that Hannah expected love to "just happen," and was putting the burden of making the sparks fly entirely on the man. Everyone knows that a match can't light on its own— it needs a little friction. I knew that it would take time for her to open up enough for a connection to be possible. Hoping that, in time, chemistry would develop, I suggested that Hannah consider going on second dates with men whom she thought were a good fit, even if she didn't feel a strong initial connection. In the end, she chose not to take my coaching, and her membership ran out. I bumped into her a few months ago and, after five years, she was still waiting for the lightning.

How could I have been so wrong about both of these women and their odds of finding love?

Separately, we both realized that our preconceived notions were being challenged. Together, we began searching for answers.

In the years to come, patterns would emerge as we watched our clients go through the dating process. Still, it would take years for all of the Predictors to reveal themselves to us.

As matchmakers, we have a front row seat to the dating dramas being played out before our eyes. Few people can offer the insights that our over 30 years of combined experience have given us. We have seen all aspects of the dating world, whereas the individual person is only privy to his or her own experience. We hear both sides of every date and know the entire story. We've placed ourselves in the thick of it and watched the triumphs and tragedies of thousands of love stories unfold. As professional matchmakers, we are in the trenches with singles, working on their behalf, partnering with them, guiding them, consoling them, and championing them. Through it all, we've been searching for the answer to our burning question: "Why do some people find love, while others don't?" Time and time again, we noticed that our most successful clients were similar in a number of ways. Ultimately, we realized it was their *approach* to dating that had the common factors— six, in fact. Those factors are The Six Predictors of Dating Success!

The Six Predictors of Dating Success

The Priority Predictor – Make your search for love a central part of your life. Let it take precedence, and give it the attention it deserves.

The Belief Predictor – Know that love is attainable for you. Nurture your inner truth. Know that a person who is right for you exists and that you will have the ability to find them.

The Open Predictor – Love is looking for you, so be open to how it shows up. Free yourself from the constraints of your preconceived ideals and allow love to surprise you.

The Balance Predictor – Protect yourself from the extreme highs and lows of dating. Foster and maintain emotional balance by keeping your perspective as you navigate the delights and disappointments throughout the process.

The Vehicle Predictor – Give love a way to find you and give yourself a way to find love. To reach your destination, you need a means of getting there. Make use of a variety of vehicles for meeting other great single people.

The Action Predictor – Take action— find love. Move yourself from thinking about finding love to actually doing it. Bring Action to all of the other Predictors so that they can reach their full potential.

WHERE IS LOVE ON YOUR LIST?
THE PRIORITY PREDICTOR

WHERE IS LOVE ON YOUR LIST?
THE PRIORITY PREDICTOR

"Nothing happens until you decide. Make a decision and watch your life move forward."

–Oprah

CONVENTIONAL WISDOM – *Also known as "advice," and when it is bad it can be dangerous!*

"You want to buy your dream house? Just relax, stop looking so hard and the right house will come along." Said no one, ever.

Buying a home is one of the most important goals in a person's life. Let's say you wanted to become a homeowner, and you were in the process of searching for a wonderful house. If your realtor called to tell you she had found just what you were looking for, wouldn't you drop everything to go see it right away? Of course you would! We all know that a certain amount of flexibility is required in the home buying process. You need to be ready and willing to change plans or rearrange your schedule to visit a property. Wouldn't choosing to skip a social event in order to make a bid on your dream house seem like an obvious choice? In other words, if you want to buy a home, then the search for the right house takes precedence over other activities because it is such an important goal. Can you imagine telling someone that the only way to find their dream home was not to look for it? At best this would be laughed at and quickly ignored. At worst, it is bad advice, and bad advice can be dangerous.

Buying a home, losing weight, building a career, etc. We all have a list of important life goals that we know require our time, energy, and dedication. Why is it that finding love is so often left off that list? Isn't love just as important as a nice place to live? Isn't finding love as vital as a healthy body, or a rewarding job? Of course it is! So, why is it that, when it comes to love, we are willing to listen when people say, "Don't try so hard. When you stop looking for love, that's when you'll find it?"

If love is vital, we need to commit ourselves to finding it. **We need to make the search for love a priority.**

Misconceptions about Finding Love – It Doesn't "Just Happen"

More often than not, finding love takes a back seat to other concerns. While most people want love in their lives, they are led to believe that love should be a secondary pursuit and feel pressured to give their attention to seemingly more pressing matters. Wanting to be perceived as level-headed, mature, and responsible, they succumb to modern society's message that tells them actively looking for love is frivolous and desperate. As a result, the search for love is rarely designated as important enough to be a priority.

Along with the message that looking for love is silly and impractical, we are also fed a modern myth that finding love is something that should "just happen." Hollywood has a lot to answer for in the creation and perpetuation of this mindset. In fact, much of our culture's romantic tradition is built upon the illusion that Hollywood promotes. The entertainment industry trades in romantic propaganda. It produces comedies that make us believe love will bump into us on a crowded street or simply fall into our laps. It's a fantasy world and is quite harmless, as long as we keep it in the realm of *fantasy* and separate from *reality*.

Much like the entertainment industry, society conditions us from a young age by perpetuating the myth that love is a magical occurrence and something that just happens with no rhyme or reason. We grow up with this message all around us: from the enchanting fairytales, to oversimplified family stories of how people met, to advertising that sells products by reducing the pursuit of love to a single romantic moment. We are led to believe that love is something you only get if you are fortunate. It turns love into a lottery, where only the lucky win.

Inevitably, we end up thinking that we have no power or influence over this important part of our lives. We are nearly brainwashed to think that actively searching for love will make us desperate, misguided, weak, and old-fashioned. So, when we *do* decide to take matters into our own hands, the typical reaction from those around us can be damaging. Relatives and friends may be well-meaning advisors when it comes to matters of the heart, but more often than not, those who feel that they are in a position to offer advice are the wrong people to listen to. Many are in long-term relationships, which is great for them, but it doesn't mean they understand your situation. It may have been decades since they last dated and, in that time, a lot has changed in the dating world. Single friends, who date a lot, may think that they are offering expert advice. However, their vast dating experience does not make them experts at being *successful* in finding love.

Close friends, family, and even the media consistently reinforce the idea that finding love is something that will *just happen*. They imply that finding a life partner is something we simply have trust in or believe in, as if it were a simple question of fate. But it's not! Be selective in who you take advice from. Dating is like anything else. Good information can make for smooth sailing, and bad information can sink your ship.

Another reason why we can't leave love to luck and chance is that the social makeup of our environment changes drastically over time. When we are in our teens and early 20's, everyone in our social group is usually around our age and single. Then, in our mid- to late 20's, more and more people have paired off. Add increasing job and personal responsibilities, and most people have less and less free time to socialize. With friends getting married, having children, and losing interest in the singles scene, our social options begin to dry up. By the time we enter our 30's, our social circles contain fewer singles, and our opportunities to organically meet people dwindle even further. As our dating environment changes and we struggle to meet new people, we must give finding a partner more precedence and a higher priority. Otherwise, we will have little or no chance to meet good candidates and find love.

So, cast aside that notion that love falls from the sky. Chase off the chubby little cherub that is Cupid. Love is not something we can leave to chance. If you know that you want love, a life partner, and even a family, it is vital that you give yourself the OK to make your search for love a priority. See it as a good choice. See that you are setting yourself up to reach your life goals and the future you want. How can anyone call that desperate?

If you know you want love in your life, make finding love your priority.

Making Room for Love

We want you to pause here, take a moment, and ask yourself,

"Am I ready for love?"

It may sound like an odd question, to which the immediate answer will be, "Of course I'm ready for love!" But take a moment to consider what finding love means . . . think about how it will change your life. Think about your routines, your leisure time, and your quiet time. Are you ready to let someone else into those areas? Are you ready to share your life?

If the answer is, "Yes" (and we can almost hear you shouting, "YES!"), then read on.

Making a Commitment to Yourself

To reiterate, the decision to make love a priority in your life is a smart choice. More than that, making love a priority is a *necessity* if you wish to succeed. So, let's look at what making your search for love a priority actually means. A priority is a conscious commitment to take actions that will achieve a specific goal. Education, better health, secure finances— most of us have made one, or all, of these goals a priority at some point in our lives. In making them a priority, we committed to taking actual steps toward a tangible result. Finding love is no different. It is not enough to simply tell yourself that finding love is now a priority in your life. Priority demands consistent application and follow through, otherwise it is little more than a wish and a hope.

We are always perplexed when clients tell us that finding a life partner is their primary goal, yet refuse to make the necessary adjustments in their lives to reach that goal. Like buying a home, applying for a job, or losing weight, you need to adjust the other areas of your life so that they don't impede your goal of finding love. Making one part of your life a priority means that the other areas must align with your goal. If you are unwilling to make adjustments in your life, then you are not truly making love a priority.

There are times in your life when you may decide that other concerns are more important than dating. It is fine to make that decision— just be sure you are making it from an informed position and are fully conscious of what it means for the long term. If you decide to put other wants, needs, and considerations ahead of dating, know that your goal of finding love is likely to suffer. A number of years ago, we had a client named Ian whose story illustrates how making love a priority means making adjustments in your life.

Ian – Getting Real

Almost everyone wants love, but not everyone is ready to make love a priority. Take Ian. When we met him, our first thought was, this is going to be easy. Ian was 35 years old and a law enforcement officer. He was tall and exceptionally handsome. He worked out, but not obsessively, and he was fit and well-built. Ian was also confident. He exuded an air of self-assurance that could put anyone at ease. When we sat down to talk, he told us that what he needed, more than anything, was to find love. Ian wanted to find his soul mate. He wanted to meet a woman with integrity, whose beauty wasn't only wrapped up in her appearance. He wanted to marry, raise a family, and live the happily-ever-after life he felt he deserved. We felt he deserved it, too.

However, it didn't take long for us to realize that something was wrong. Dates did not go well, and our follow-up calls to him went unanswered. When we brought Ian into the office to find out what was going on, the truth came out. He confessed that, when he wasn't on a date we arranged, he was spending his weekends out at the clubs. With his good looks and charm, Ian was a sure-fire hit with the ladies, and he enjoyed it. He enjoyed it far too much. With a little coaxing, Ian finally admitted that he could not stop picking up women in bars and clubs. He told us that these women were the precise opposite of the woman he'd asked us to look for. They were not what he considered "marriage material."

Now, you may say that Ian had not been honest with us, but the essential point here was that Ian had not been honest with himself about what it would take to find real love. Outwardly, he wanted love, marriage, family— inwardly, he didn't want to give up playing the field, one-night stands, and non-commitment. He was still reaching for the short-term pleasures. Although he said he wanted to find love, his actions showed us that he wasn't willing to make his search a priority. If he was willing, the weekend hook-ups would have stopped. Ian's choice to continue indulging in these casual flings seemed harmless to him. However, it was undermining the dates we arranged and preventing him from connecting emotionally with any of the women. It was costing him the love and happiness he longed for. He needed to shift his lifestyle to make his goals of love and marriage a priority.

The Big and the Small Adjustments

Generally, people resist change. We know and understand this fact. We also know that, for love to come into someone's life, change of some sort is inevitable. Change is part of making the search for love a priority. However, we often experience resistance when we encourage change. We encounter people who say that they are dedicated to finding love, only to discover that they are unwilling to give up habits or attachments that hinder their search.

Sometimes, like Ian, clients need to make big changes. For example, on more than one occasion, we have been at an impasse with people who refuse to adjust their schedules to make room for dating and social events. Other times, the changes we ask our clients to make are small tweaks in their habits or preferences. These smaller changes are no less important or impactful. For instance, we sometimes suggest that a client make changes in his or her image and personal presentation. Dating is a facet of life where you need to look *your* best. We wouldn't be doing our jobs if we didn't help our clients highlight their best attributes in all areas, including the way that they look. While we are always considerate and tactful when dealing with someone's appearance, there are certain things we cannot ignore. Examples: shapeless clothes; unisex outfits; comb-over hairstyles on men; short, masculine haircuts on women. By all means, feel comfortable with your style! However, it is imperative to take into consideration what a potential partner will find attractive. The priority of finding love must trump your affinity for a particular look. Ask yourself, "Is this hairstyle more important than finding happiness and love?"

We once worked with a woman who insisted that she would only date exceptionally tall men. *OK*, we thought, this is her preference. This is what she wants in a man. When we asked her why height was so important to her, she told us that she liked to wear high heels, and not just high heels, but four or five inch stilettos, and any man she dated would need to be taller than her when they went out. "Wait a minute," we said, "stop and think about this." The average American man is five feet, nine-and-a-half inches tall. Thanks to her predilection for stilettos, she was cutting out an enormous percentage of the male population, and missing out on meeting many amazing men who could be ideal matches. We put it to her straight: "What is more important to you— that you get to wear stilettos, or that you find love and happiness?" When put into such stark terms, the question allowed her to really think about what the true priority was in her life.

A New Way of Thinking

Establishing a new priority isn't just about making tweaks and changes. It involves adopting a new way of thinking— one that is conscious, aware, and moves you toward your goal. To demonstrate this concept, we would like to give you the example of Katherine whose story shows the significance of even the small choices we make in daily life. Let's join Katherine on her lunch break.

Katherine – Out to Lunch

Katherine is picking up lunch at the deli. There are a few people in line ahead of her, and the customer being served just made a long and complicated order. Knowing that she's going to be there for a while, she takes out her phone and checks Facebook. Completely unaware of her surroundings, Katherine doesn't notice that the cute guy from the third floor of her building just walked through the door. She reads her Facebook news feed until it is her turn to order. Never looking up from her phone for more than a couple of seconds, she orders, pays, gets her food, and leaves. She is halfway out the door before she notices that the cute guy is there, and she has missed her chance to talk to him.

What if Katherine had resisted the urge to occupy herself with Facebook? What if she had stayed present in the real world where she could make a connection with a flesh-and-blood human being? What if Katherine began looking around the deli? What if she had noticed that the cute guy from the third floor was in line behind her? She could have made eye contact, smiled, and said hello, creating that all important first connection with someone she found attractive. She could have actively put her search for love ahead of something as inconsequential as a Facebook update. What if you made your search for love a priority? How many more connections could you make?

Be conscious of how you choose to interact with the world. Know that every decision you make has a consequence and an effect on your life. Be mindful that choosing to retreat into your phone won't get you any closer to finding love, while interacting with someone in the real world could lead to a conversation and a new connection.

Shift your way of thinking so that you can maximize your chances of meeting someone. Big changes in your life can be made in very simple ways and at basic levels. Consider yourself in this situation: after a long day of work, a friend invites you out for the evening. What if, instead of framing the offer as another drain on your already zapped energy, you think of going out as an opportunity to move your goals forward? Instead of choosing to stay at home and collapse on the sofa, you decide to accept the invitation— you never know who you might meet: a friend of a friend, or someone new. You've made the choice, knowing that, instead of putting love on the back burner, you are honoring your priority and moving yourself toward your goal. Choosing to be social is just one of the small ways you can significantly increase your odds of meeting someone.

So, once again, we want you to look inside yourself. We want you to get to the heart of what you want and what you are ready for, and drop all pretense. Are you ready for love?

Yes?

Good!

Getting in the Mood

"Mood" is a very old word. It comes from the Old English mōd, which means "mind" or "spirit." Interestingly enough, it also means courage.

When it comes to finding love, mood is paramount.

How are you feeling today? Positive, negative, indifferent, confused?

Sometimes a whole range of emotions can flash through us in an instant. Other times, one feeling can dominate us for days or weeks. We know these mental states as moods. Good mood, bad mood, silly mood, serious mood. We are moody creatures.

We all know what it feels like to be at the mercy of our mood. Most of us believe we have about as much power to change our mood as we do to change the weather. However, we do have influence over how we feel. Sure, you may not be able to make yourself feel happy in an instant, but you can point yourself in that direction one thought at a time. You can make it easier for happiness to arrive; or optimism, or playfulness, or whatever mood you wish to experience.

You have to be in the right mood to answer when opportunity knocks. And if you aren't, you need to find the courage to change your mood and open the door.

Lauren – I'll Think About That Tomorrow

When we met Lauren, she was 42 years old. She had blonde hair, a svelte figure, and a beautiful face with a warm smile that was quick to appear. She was down to earth and sporty, yet feminine and sophisticated. Most people would have wondered why she needed help with her love life at all. But by the time we met Lauren, we knew from our experience that regardless of someone's looks, charm, or success, people still need help finding love.

After sorting through a large field of potential introductions, we chose Ethan. He was in his mid-forties, friendly, masculine, and a gentleman. He led a very busy life. Not only was Ethan the CEO of a corporation, he was also a widower and a dedicated father to his two children. Despite his full set of commitments, Ethan was determined to find love again and had made room in his life for his search. He was an ideal candidate for Lauren. When we told these two about each other, they were both excited. We saw a fairytale ending in the making.

Lauren and Ethan went out on a date. They chose a little restaurant in one of the city's historic districts. It was a beautiful summer evening, and they sat at a small table outside. With the lights twinkling above their heads, they laughed, they talked, and they shared stories. Ethan was, in no uncertain terms, hooked. He wanted to see more of this beautiful and intelligent woman. For her part, Lauren reported back to us that she found him handsome and easy to talk to. She told us she felt the sparks of a real connection.

We were excited to talk with Ethan and tell him he could call Lauren to ask her out on a second date. We knew he would.

A few weeks later, we caught up with him and asked how things with Lauren were progressing. We were sure they were seeing each other regularly and that a relationship had already begun. Imagine our surprise when Ethan's face fell as he told us a second date had never happened.

"Didn't you call?" we asked.

"Yes, of course I called."

"And???"

When he called, he got her voicemail. He left a message, expressing how much he had enjoyed their first date and how he wanted to see her again.

"Then what happened?"

"Nothing."

Excited to connect with her, he had anticipated her call that evening or the next day. He waited. Two days went by. Still nothing. Three days after he'd left the message, Lauren finally called him back. She got his voicemail, and it was her turn to leave a message. A day later, Ethan called her— and so the extended game of phone tag continued. In the end, Ethan simply gave up.

"I don't think this is going anywhere," he said. "I think it's time to meet someone else."

Confused, we arranged to meet with Lauren so that we could hear her side of the story. What she told us was a pretty familiar tale.

Yes, Lauren had thoroughly enjoyed her evening with Ethan, and yes, she was hoping for a second date. When Ethan called, it was just before nine o'clock. That evening, Lauren was tired. This was not unusual as her work schedule had her up early every morning and often in bed by nine. When the phone rang, she didn't pick up. Wanting to get to bed and knowing it wouldn't be a quick conversation, she let it go to voicemail. Lauren listened to his message, decided she would call back the following day, and went off to bed. The next day, she was feeling a little flat when she got home from work. She knew she should call Ethan, but she wasn't in the mood and decided it would be easier to just call tomorrow.

When tomorrow rolled around, she once again put off making the call. Eventually she did pick up the phone and ended up getting his voicemail. By the time Ethan listened to her voicemail, after so many days without hearing from her, the energy he had previously felt had diminished, causing her message to sound short and lackluster. Accordingly, when Ethan called back and yet again got her voicemail, his message reflected his waning interest and faltering determination. And so it goes. All the excitement, the feeling of delight that both parties had felt, was allowed to fizzle out over a few brief recorded messages.

After hearing the story, it was clear to us that Lauren had let her potential happiness slip through her fingers. Sure, you may say, she was tired, she'd been working hard, and she couldn't have known it would all hinge on not picking up the phone then and there. But it did. When Ethan made the first call and she decided not to answer, Lauren didn't just let him down— she let herself down, too.

The reason Lauren didn't pick up the phone was that she was too tired and wanted to get to bed so that she could be fresh for work in the morning. The simple fact was that Lauren had not made finding love a priority in her life. After such a great first date, and a definite spark with a wonderful man, she chose to wait. What if the following night, despite feeling worn out, she had given herself a little push and attempted to change her mood? She could have made the call, and in simply speaking with him, she could have reignited the magic of their first date. Even though she was interested, Ethan had no way of knowing. He figured that his interest was one-sided. She dropped the torch, and he moved on. This is why mood is so important, and why being conscious of your mood matters.

If you're not in the mood, you're not in the game.

Olivia – Save the Date

Olivia was 42 years-old, divorced, and came to us with the hope of finding love again. She had a kind heart and a joyful nature that never failed to see the best in every situation. As for looks, she was average— not the kind of woman who stood out in a crowd. A nurse practitioner in a busy practice, Olivia talked about her job with the kind of passion that made it clear she loved her work. Her commitment to her patients was inspiring, but left us concerned by the extraordinary amount of her time and energy that was wrapped up in her career. When we took her on, we explained to her that we expected our clients to make finding love a major priority. She told us that it was.

The truth is, we didn't expect Olivia to make room in her life for dating. We hoped she would, but knowing how much of her life she devoted to her work, we were prepared to be let down. We couldn't have been more wrong.

Olivia made the most of every opportunity. If we had someone we thought she should meet, she quickly made room in her schedule and enthusiastically went on the date. She had fun, and because she was enjoying herself, so did the men she dated. On the only occasion that an emergency forced her to reschedule a date, she made sure to do so right away.

It was no surprise that Olivia found love. One day, she came to visit us and showed us her engagement ring. She lavished us with hugs and praised our work. Quietly, pointedly, we let her know that her success was her own— we had simply fulfilled our part of the bargain by coaching her, introducing her to men, and arranging the dates. It was her attitude that was the real triumph.

Although she worked hard and loved her job, Olivia knew how important finding love was to her. Thanks to this knowledge, she was able to prioritize her life to reach her goal. She's still married, she's still happy, and she still maintains a healthy balance between her work and her personal life.

When we take on a client, we don't expect them to clear their calendars for the next few years. We don't imagine that every waking minute will be spent working on finding love. That would be unhealthy and detrimental. What we do expect, as we told Olivia, is that if they are serious about finding love, their search needs to be a top priority.

It's not just your work that has to accommodate your search for love. Your social life also needs to be flexible. Do you spend every Friday night with your friends? If a potential life-partner invites you to an event that conflicts with your weekly plans, what should you do? The Priority Predictor would tell you to explain to your friends that you will see them next week, and go on the date. We aren't suggesting that your friendships aren't important. We are simply reminding you that finding love trumps your weekly evening out. Making your search for love a priority means that the other areas of your life need to be flexible to support it. Do you have a spinning class every Thursday evening? If it clashes with a hot date, you know which one should be your priority. Go to a morning class, or run at lunch time.

We are not saying that you should set aside everything else in your life. Without a full and interesting life, you stop being a full and interesting person. But the important point is this: make room for dating. Make it your priority.

Making Love a Priority

We've seen why prioritizing your search for love is important. It's not just about deciding to put dating at the top of your to-do list. You need to weigh the decisions you make in the other areas of your life against your goal of finding love. From the seemingly insignificant decisions to the obviously important ones, you need to ask yourself, "Will doing this take me closer to my goal or further away from it?" By consistently evaluating your actions in light of your objective, you will be able to stay focused and keep your search for love at the forefront of your mind.

Emma – Embracing Priority

Emma's story is a perfect example of how important the Priority Predictor is in your search for love. It's a story of pain, of happiness found, happiness lost, and love's eventual triumph.

Some years ago, Emma was in a comfortable, satisfying relationship. At the time, she was in her mid-thirties, emotionally happy, and professionally secure. She was a woman who felt assured that her life was on the right track. One evening, her boyfriend Michael took her out for dinner. It was a special and romantic evening at an elegant restaurant with delicious food and fine wine. Throughout the meal, Michael couldn't hide his knowing smile. When the desserts were finished and the last of the wine had been poured, Michael suddenly became very serious. From his pocket, he produced a small, red velvet box. With her heart fluttering, Emma watched as he got up from his chair, went down on one knee, and opened the box. Inside was the ring she had always dreamed of.

"Yes," she said as tears filled her eyes and her heart felt like it was exploding. "Yes, yes, yes!"

Life following the proposal was, of course, different. Emma thoroughly enjoyed planning the wedding, choosing the invitations, and finding the perfect dress. It couldn't get any better than this.

Then, one day, from out of nowhere, Michael destroyed her world. He suddenly broke off the engagement. Mumbling something about compatibility and his uncertainty, with shocking ease, he bowed out of her life forever.

Emma went into freefall. Her life was shattered. The future, once bright and exciting, had become a terrifying place. Slowly, hesitantly, she began to pick up the pieces. She threw herself into her job. Emma had always been a devoted professional, but now, her work had become a life raft. After a year of hard work and quiet sadness, Emma decided enough was enough. It was time for her to lift her head and face the world as a single person looking for love.

When Emma met with us, she told us her story. Full of positive energy and gifted with an enormous and compassionate heart, we immediately knew she was someone we were excited to work with. As we got to know Emma, we realized that she was the kind of woman who made her goals a reality. From running half-marathons to advocating for members of her community, her positive and determined approach to life helped her reach any goal she set for herself. Professionally, she had become a vice president at an international company. Her take-charge attitude and straightforward, authoritative way of speaking were tools for success in her career, but worked against her in the world of dating.

Love was the one area of her life where she hadn't reached her goals. We asked Emma to tell us about her most recent date. What she described sounded more like a business dinner. She had worn a conservative gray pants suit and had spent the hour and a half vetting the man for compatibility. We could see that, for Emma, making love a priority meant making changes.

The proactive person that she was, she agreed to do whatever was necessary. However, when we suggested softening her attitude and approach to dating, she couldn't see how it would be an advantage. "A modern successful woman needs to be tough to succeed," she told us. "Believe me, I've learned the hard way."

We agreed that, in the world of business, in the male-dominated boardroom, she needed to be strong, bold, and make assertive arguments, but dating is not the same. If she was all hard shell, any potential partner would simply bounce off or grow tired of trying to get beneath the surface. Along with her drive and determination, she needed to show her warmth, kindness, and immensely giving nature. Together, both sides of her personality were an irresistible combination. On its own, her intensity made her seem like just another potential colleague. If she also allowed her warmhearted side to show, the men she met would be able to see a complete picture of who she was. They would be able to envision her as both a strong and loving potential partner.

Emma began to grasp just what it meant, for her, to make the search for love a priority. She realized that she couldn't find someone to spend her life with the same way she negotiated a merger. She began to see that, where dating was concerned, she needed to step back a little and soften her approach. We began coaching with Emma. Continuing her commitment to making love a priority and knowing that change was necessary, she learned to concentrate on connecting with her dates and enjoying the evening. She began to relax and let situations unfold.

This emotional softening helped Emma find a new openness when it came to matters of the heart. This was not a vulnerability, but rather a new maturity. It was an admission that being hurt was always a possibility, but with faith and patience, she could embrace dating as a woman of both hope and self-assurance. With these changes, Emma learned how to balance both sides of her nature and returned to the world of dating with purpose, but also with grace.

She soon began to make changes in other areas of her life that would support her goal of finding love. She created a new dynamic with her dates. She began to have fun with the dating process and see it as an enjoyable and positive experience, rather than just a means to an end. She adapted her wardrobe to bring out her femininity. She reorganized her calendar to maximize her availability for evenings out, singles events, and dates. She made the most of each experience.

About a year after she began coaching, Emma attended one of our events where she connected with a man named Alex. They talked easily and laughed a lot, and both came away feeling something special. When Emma told us she was interested in Alex, we were surprised, thrilled, and, we have to admit, a little bit vindicated. Knowing they would be a great match, we had introduced them to each other once before at a similar event. It was before Emma started her coaching. She had arrived late and left early, explaining that she was working on a big project. Her conversation with Alex had been brief and formal. When we had asked her about him later, she only vaguely remembered meeting him and had said something about him being "too nice."

This time, when Emma met Alex, she was there at the beginning of the event and had left her work behind at the office. Relaxed and having fun, she enjoyed sampling new wines and talking with new people. When Alex came up to her, she smiled and chatted comfortably with him, and by the end of the evening, they had kindled a spark and planned a first date.

A few weeks later, we met with Emma. She was beaming.

"Is he really as wonderful as he seems?" she asked us.

"Yes!" we happily assured her.

"I didn't know this kind of man existed," she admitted.

They fell in love, were engaged, planned a beautiful wedding, and started their family with a baby boy. Emma and Alex are an amazing couple who are supportive of each other's goals, hopes, and dreams.

Emma's story shows how bringing the Priority Predictor to your search for love can bring you success. Emma transformed her approach to dating, managed her mood, reorganized her calendar, and changed her personal appearance, all to realize her goal.

When you decide to make the search for love a priority, you have to understand just what this decision means for you. Look at your life. Look at your choices. Where can you make adjustments? What do you need less of, and what do you need more of? Crucially, know that you don't need to be alone in this: seek out the support of friends and family. Show them how important your search for love is and how seriously you are taking it. Ask your friends and family to accept your priority and to support you in it.

Know that every decision should be measured against your priority. Certain choices may seem inconsequential, like Lauren's decision to go to bed early and not return that phone call right away. When you set yourself on the road to finding love, everything matters, *everything*, whether big or small.

Finding someone to share your life and your love with is worth the effort! Remember that it is OK to make your desire for love a priority, and it is completely necessary, if you really want it to happen.

THE FOUNDATION OF YOUR ROMANTIC FUTURE
THE BELIEF PREDICTOR

THE FOUNDATION OF YOUR ROMANTIC FUTURE

THE BELIEF PREDICTOR

"Whether you think you can, or you think you can't—

you're right."

–Henry Ford

Tessa and Charlotte – A Tale of Two Beliefs

IT ALL started with a wrong number. We were in the office one afternoon when the phone rang. Susie answered. On the other end of the line was a woman's voice.

"Hi, is this the Cornerstone Deli?"

"No. Sorry, you must have dialed the wrong number."

"Oh. Okay, sorry to bother you."

"It's no bother at all," said Susie.

"Thanks! You know, some people can be so rude when you call the wrong number."

"There's just no need for that. I always enjoy talking to new people!"

"Anyway, just out of curiosity, what kind of business are you?"

"This is Affinity Matchmaking. We're matchmakers."

"Matchmakers? You mean you get people hooked up?"

Susie laughed. "We help people find love."

"Really? Now that's something I could use. How does it work?"

By the end of the conversation, the caller, whose name was Tessa, had confided that she'd been single for way too long, and was very much looking for love. Intrigued by our work, Tessa decided, then and there, that she'd like to come in and meet us. She wanted to see what we could do for her.

Susie, beside herself with excitement, said, "It's gotta be fate. The stars are lining up!" It was too much of a coincidence that she would call a wrong number and have it turn out to be what she was truly looking for in life. "I have a feeling this woman is going to be easy to match," said Susie with a smile.

When Tessa came to meet us, Susie's prediction seemed dead on. Tessa was simply adorable. She was in her mid thirties, about 5'2", slim, yet curvy. She wore a fabulous outfit, and her long dark curly hair cascaded over her shoulders and halfway down her back. Her round face was pretty and her smile delightful, but it was her eyes that really brought all of her features together. They were wide, bright, intelligent eyes, richly brown, dark, enticing, and alert. When Tessa looked at you, you got the feeling that you were getting special attention from a special person. And as if the physical attributes weren't enough, she had a brain to match— Tessa was a cardiologist.

So, to recap, Tessa had found us by a seemingly fateful accident. She was beautiful and approachable, professional and smart, and she was looking for love. We didn't think we would have much trouble finding her a great match.

Wanting to get a feel for the kind of woman she was, we encouraged Tessa to tell us about herself. What we heard was something of a shock. It turned out that Tessa came from a culture where marriage and having children were the end-all and be-all of what it meant to be a woman. What's more, in that particular tradition, a woman was expected to be married and have started a family by her mid-twenties, at the latest. Anything else was considered a failure.

As she spoke, we watched some of the light go out of Tessa's eyes. Here she was, halfway through her thirties. She hadn't married, she hadn't had children, and without a boyfriend, she wasn't even close. She told us that she saw herself as a disappointment to her family. We could practically see the weight of her belief in the slump of her shoulders. "Wait a second, this doesn't make sense!" we told her. "Let's look at what you're saying." We pointed out that she was a bold and intelligent woman, who had made her own way in the world and established herself as a woman of independence and strength. We enthusiastically reminded her that she was in a profession that demands a formidable mind, a strong character, and a caring nature. Tessa was no failure, and we were determined to prove it. We took her on as a client.

Around the same time, we also met a woman named Charlotte. She was divorced and in her late-forties. She was a successful consultant who, for the last fifteen years, had led a very busy life. Along with working hard at her job, she had been a devoted single mother, raising her son by herself. Now, her son was off at college and starting to find his own path in life. As an empty-nester, Charlotte was finally realizing that, between her son and her job, her personal life had been on hold. It was time to put *herself* first for once. She decided what was missing was love, and she wanted our help to find it.

Charlotte had a kind and lovely nature that was apparent as soon as we met her. Having been a busy single mom for most of her adult life, it had been a long time since her appearance had made her list of major concerns. She was tall and heavyset. Her dull salt and pepper hair was cut very short, and to accommodate her busy schedule, she didn't style it at all and just let the tight curls do what they wanted. She didn't wear makeup, and her unflattering wardrobe was filled with boxy business suits in a range of muted colors.

When we agreed to take her on as a client, we laid out the changes we expected from her. To begin with, she needed to restrict the masculine wardrobe to work days and rediscover her femininity. And by femininity, we did not mean the "mom" look, which was her other default style. We suggested that she should grow out her hair. While we could see how her job had dictated her clothing in her male dominated profession, we needed her to redefine her persona for her personal life: from a hard-edged professional to one that was relaxed and feminine. Our goal was for her to develop a look that would help her connect with and attract men, not compete with them.

Charlotte listened to our ideas with an expression of bemused skepticism. But knowing that this was our area of expertise, she took our recommendations. She agreed to go shopping and change her hairstyle. Following our discussion, she remembered how much she enjoyed having beautiful long hair and wearing clothes that made her feel pretty. Charlotte realized she might really enjoy this.

Meanwhile, we were still working with Tessa. Setting up her dates was turning out to be just as easy as we thought it would be. Men were always excited to meet her. We sent her on several introductions, and after a few weeks, we checked back with her to see how things were going. "Everything is great!" she said. "I've met some really nice guys, and had some fun evenings." She told us that one man she had gone to dinner with was exactly the kind of person she had been hoping for. He was handsome, funny, and attentive. They had gone to a Thai restaurant, eaten a delicious meal, and then went for a drink to continue the evening. They had talked for hours and planned to see each other again. Feeling satisfied and confident that she would connect with one of the men we introduced her to, we let things take their course.

Charlotte was a different matter. We did get her out on a few dates, and she said she had a nice time, but nothing came of them. In talking to her, we got the impression that she felt out of place on her dates. We could see that this uncomfortable feeling was keeping her from enjoying the experience and making connections. We decided to encourage Charlotte and give her tools that would help her feel more comfortable expressing herself on dates. When she came to see us, we told her what we thought was holding her back. She listened, as she always did, with that curious half smile. We got the impression that she was humoring us. Yet, when we had said our piece, she was in total agreement. She said she would be open to coaching, and agreed to attend our flirting class and take dance lessons.

After some coaching and a few classes, we asked her to attend a few of our mixers. We were pleased to see that, at each of the events, Charlotte got a lot of attention and was very social. It was not unusual to find her talking to one, two, or even three men at a time. They seemed to be drawn to her.

As the months passed, things with Tessa began to change. We started to notice the strangest thing happening over and over. After one or two dates, things seemed to fall apart. Either Tessa or the man she was seeing would suddenly cancel plans. There were any number of excuses: he had a work event he couldn't get out of, he wasn't feeling well, or he had a family emergency. When Tessa withdrew from a pre-arranged date, her excuses, like those of the men, were less than convincing. It was time for us to find out what was going on.

We decided to speak with Jeffrey, one of the men we had introduced to Tessa. We knew we could count on him to tell us exactly what was happening. He had been on three dates with her, and what he had to say was quite a surprise.

Yes, Tessa was a very good-looking woman. She was warm, funny, and friendly. The first date had been great, with lots of honest and interesting conversation, interspersed with plenty of laughter. He had been eager to set up a second date, and so had Tessa. He told us that the second date had been just as wonderful, with the same comfortable atmosphere and easy rapport between them. However, on the third date, a change started to come over Tessa. Her smile appeared less often and the laughter had dried up. Odd, uncomfortable silences began to punctuate the banter. By the end of the evening, Jeffrey was starting to question himself:

"What did I do wrong?"

"Was it something I said?"

"Was it the venue?"

"What happened?"

We asked him if he would consider trying to rescue the situation with another date. He hemmed and hawed and eventually admitted that no, he really wasn't interested in taking her out again.

We were also beginning to notice a change in our own interactions with Tessa. We started receiving distressed emails from her. In these emails, she said that dating was too much hard work. She complained that it was time-consuming and that nothing ever went anywhere. She questioned the point of it all. We called Tessa and arranged for her to come see us.

At first, she told us she was just as confused as we were about her lack of progress. She enjoyed the men's company, and came home both happy with herself and eager to see them again. Then, she explained, as the days went by, something would start bothering her. Something from deep inside. With gentle prompting, she finally admitted what she thought the problem was.

Tessa could not get over the feeling that she was a failure. It was her old fears resurfacing— she was in her mid-thirties and she still had not found love, still had not gotten married, still had no children. Each date was sabotaged by her fear that either she wasn't good enough for them or that they wouldn't be good enough for her. Her beliefs were still preventing her from getting into a relationship. Even though she had met several wonderful men, she could not escape the inherent idea that she had, and always would, fall short of what was expected of her.

It didn't matter what we said. We were fighting against a belief that was so deeply ingrained, only she could shift it. And she wasn't ready to do that. Tessa told us she needed to take a break from dating. We knew she had lost hope. We were sad to see her set her dreams aside. There had been so much potential, and there still was! It's not in our nature to give up, and we told Tessa that, when she was ready to start dating again, we would be here.

About a year later, we were talking with a mutual friend who had known Tessa for years. We asked how Tessa was doing. The friend told us that Tessa was still single and had confessed that she simply did not believe she would ever find love.

It turned out that Tessa had felt this all along. Even during those first happy, exciting dates, there was an inescapable voice within her saying the same thing, over and over: "You can't find love. You're a failure." And so, Tessa had sabotaged her own happiness. Her feelings of failure and inferiority had prevented her from moving forward. It was a self-fulfilling prophecy. She believed it, therefore she made it true. Soon after Tessa stopped working with us, she moved to another part of the country. Last we heard, she still hadn't realized her hopes of finding love and having a family. We never got the chance to work with Tessa again. We wish she had given us the opportunity to help her overcome her negative beliefs and cultivate the empowering beliefs that could have made the difference. When someone is burdened with the kind of negative beliefs that can prevent them from finding love, it doesn't have to mean an unhappy ending for their story. As we will discuss later in this chapter, people have the power to change their beliefs. In transforming their beliefs, they can create the future they desire.

In the meantime, we hadn't seen Charlotte in few months, and were eager to catch up. Over the phone, she told us that she was finally ready for her trip to the hairstylist. We arranged for her to meet us at the office and then we would take her out for a complete makeover.

Elizabeth was on her phone when Charlotte arrived at the office. Covering the mouthpiece, Elizabeth whispered that she wouldn't be long and motioned for Charlotte to take a seat. It was immediately obvious that something was different about Charlotte. She was beaming and seemed almost giddy with excitement! Elizabeth quickly finished her telephone call and hung up. "Hi! What's going on? You look very excited."

Without a word, Charlotte got up, walked over, and slapped her left hand on the desk. Elizabeth looked down and saw the ring. Charlotte said, "I'm engaged!" She was radiant with excitement and happiness.

Elizabeth was thrilled. "Ahhhhhhhhhhhhhhhhhhhhhhhhh! Charlotte, I'm so happy for you!" exclaimed Elizabeth. "I can't wait to hear all about him! How did this happen so fast?"

Hearing the screams of celebration and not wanting to miss out on the action, Susie rushed into the room. "What on earth is going on in here?" Susie asked as she flung open the door. Once everyone calmed down, Charlotte told us the full story. A couple of weeks after we'd last seen her, Charlotte had attended a singles event downtown that we'd suggested she go to. Even though she didn't know anyone there, she was soon meeting men and talking with them. It had not been long before a nice man asked her to dance, and they spent the rest of the evening chatting. At the end of the night, he'd asked for her number. She'd been happy to give it. They began dating, and quickly realized they had a great deal in common and made each other really happy. Within 12 weeks, he had proposed and Charlotte had joyfully accepted.

"And I still want to go for that makeover," said Charlotte, smiling her funny smile. "Only now it's not to help me find a boyfriend. Now, it will be for my wedding!"

A few weeks after their wedding, Charlotte paid another visit to our office to show us the wedding photos. We flipped through the album, oohing and awing over the flowers and her dress. Seeing this all happen so quickly for her made us wonder what it was that had made the difference for Charlotte. Here was a woman who had been out of the dating world for fifteen years; a woman who had ignored romance, sensuality, and the desire for a relationship for so long. Now, she sat in front of us, married and deeply in love. Based on our old way of thinking, we expected Charlotte to be the kind of person who would struggle in her search for love. We had to know what her frame of mind was when she decided to look for love. Elizabeth asked her, "Charlotte, what did you think was going to happen when you started dating again?" Charlotte smiled with a vague shrug, and said, "Well, I always *knew* I was going to meet someone. I just had to figure out where the men were!"

Seven years down the road, Charlotte is still married, still happy, and still sure that she knew all along she would find a wonderful man.

Beliefs Are Powerful

Our experiences with Tessa and Charlotte led us to a powerful realization: **a person's deepest held beliefs are the *foundation* for their search for love.** Tessa believed she would never find love, so no matter what we did, there was no way to help her build a successful relationship on her faulty foundation. Charlotte was certain that love was in her future, so when we gave her the tools, she was able to build a happy and loving relationship on her strong foundation.

Belief— Emotion— Result

What you believe dictates your emotions— emotions impact how you interact with the world— how you interact with the world gives you your results.

Let's examine this idea in more detail.

What you believe dictates your emotions. If you consider the world a cold, heartless place, devoid of love and happiness, it's a fair bet that you are going to fall prey to corresponding emotions: despair, loneliness, hopelessness. Alternatively, if you see the world as being full of warmth, love, and care, you will experience comparable feelings. Let's say you are out at an event for single professionals. Your intention for the evening is to make new connections. If you believe that most of the people in the singles pool lie about something, whether it's their age, marital status, or intentions, then what will your emotions be? You will likely experience feelings of mistrust, fear, defensiveness, or at the very least, apprehension. If you believe that there are plenty of kind, open, honest people in the singles pool, then you will likely feel excited, hopeful, confident, or at least receptive.

Emotions impact how you interact with the world. To put it another way, our feelings influence and give rise to our actions. Let's go back to the singles event. If you are feeling fear, mistrust, defensiveness, or apprehension, when someone comes up to talk with you, these emotions will show in the way you greet them. Your tone may be unfriendly, your answers to their questions short, the expression on your face cold or uninterested, and your demeanor detached. If you are feeling excited, hopeful, confident, or receptive, then your smile will be warm and inviting, the tone of your voice friendly, your responses to questions engaging, and your demeanor approachable.

How you interact with the world gives you your results. It is through our actions that we connect with the world and that others experience us. Therefore, the outcome you experience in any given situation is the direct result of your actions. If you are detached when you meet new people, it is unlikely that they will be interested in getting to know you. If you are engaging, you will have the chance to make a new connection.

If you think your beliefs are invisible, you are wrong. They are very visible. Your beliefs are expressed in your verbal communication, your body language, and in the actions you take and don't take. They dictate how you interact with people and have a direct correlation to how you are perceived by others. Therefore, your beliefs impact your results, be it merely enjoying your day at work, or finding a life partner.

Let's look at the story of a former client named Sophie, whose empowering belief created positive emotions, that dictated constructive actions, and resulted in her finding love.

Sophie – "Boys Like Me"

One of our happiest experiences in matchmaking was with Sophie. Her basic belief was, "Boys *like* me." It was as simple as that. And did it work? Did it ever!

Sophie didn't consider herself a gorgeous woman. She described herself as, "Cute enough, even with my mousy hair and extra pounds." However, her simple belief that men wanted to be with her became her reality. Every time we sent her out on a date with a man, he came back telling us he couldn't wait to see her again. The feedback was always the same. She was friendly, kind, easy to talk to, and she made them feel comfortable. She nearly always got a second date and more.

Sophie got along particularly well with one of the men we sent her out with. His name was Gabe. We had introduced them because of their similar commitments to faith and family. Sophie and Gabe started seeing each other regularly. After about six months, Gabe began talking about marriage and took her to look at engagement rings. Knowing he was planning to propose, Sophie took some time to consider a future with him. She thought long and hard about it. Yes, she liked Gabe. Yes, they got along well. But, allowing some of her concerns to temper her excitement, she realized that the way they wanted to live their day-to-day lives wasn't compatible. The differences were enough to give her pause. She was clear-headed enough to know that, over time, those incompatibilities would become magnified. She knew that in the long run, this would erode their relationship and that committing herself to a life with him was not the best thing for either of them. Her decision showed not only her intelligence and intuition, but also her courage. She turned him down. She ended the relationship. It wasn't easy. It hurt for both of them. But Sophie stuck to her decision. With her foundational belief that "boys like me," Sophie was able to let go of the wrong relationship and trust that she would eventually find the right man to share her life with.

Some time later, after allowing herself to heal, Sophie came back to us and said she was ready to start looking again. Undaunted, she returned to square one. Thanks to her inner belief and the confidence this gave her, she was able to throw herself back into dating. It didn't take long for us to find a good match for her. And guess what? He proposed, too. This time, without hesitation, she said yes. Today, Sophie is still happily married and is expecting her first child.

In our experience, Sophie's success is unprecedented. We have never had a client who received two marriage proposals from wonderful men in under one year. Her belief not only gave her the ability to connect with men, but also the courage to walk away from the wrong relationship and the patience and perseverance to find the right one.

Believe good things will happen, prepare for them, and watch for opportunities. Charlotte and Sophie were not luckier than Tessa. What Charlotte and Sophie had was a belief that they would succeed. When the opportunity of finding love presented itself on dates and at events, they were ready to seize it. On the other hand, Tessa had already shut herself off from the many opportunities in front of her. She believed she was a failure and that love wasn't her destiny, so when she was on dates with great guys who were interested in her, she was unable to recognize them as her chance for finding love.

When people believe there is someone out there for them and that they will get into a relationship, they *do*. It is their belief— not how attractive, successful, or baggage-free they are— that predicts their chances of finding love. Someone who holds a positive, uplifting belief has a clear confidence and centered quality that is palpable. They are comfortable with themselves, and it shows. These qualities that come from positive beliefs are the most attractive elements a human being can possess, and people are naturally drawn to them. Conversely, having a belief that you are not going to find love, or that you are not smart enough, or rich enough, or thin, beautiful, cool, sexy, successful, funny, outgoing enough— that shows, too.

We know that maintaining positive belief can be hard work. We know how difficult it is, in the face of disappointment, to keep believing, but it is *essential* for getting into a relationship.

Believe in yourself.

Believe in the process.

Doubts and Fears

Of course, everyone has doubts and fears; they are to be expected and are a natural part of the dating process. Some of the doubts and fears we often hear are:

"What if he doesn't want a relationship?"

"What if she only likes tall guys?"

"I'm scared I won't meet someone."

"I'm not sure I'm ready to date again."

Doubts and fears can make you question your beliefs, but they are not something to be afraid of or a reason to give up. They can feel overwhelming, but can dissipate quickly and are often fleeting. Other times, they stay with us for longer and can even resurface from time to time. Whatever the situation, remember that doubts and fears are not facts. Acknowledge them for what they are: uncertainties, questions, hesitations, and worries that are merely passing thoughts. It's important to know that doubts and fears are different from a disempowering belief and do not hold the same destructive power. Don't allow doubts and fears to take hold, because when they do, they can become disempowering beliefs.

Disempowering Beliefs

What are beliefs and how are they created? As we go through life, we make conclusions about ourselves and the world. When we decide our conclusions are the truth and hold onto them, they become our beliefs. A disempowering belief is a negative truth that *you create* for yourself that undermines your goals. As matchmakers we often hear:

"I'm never going to find love."

"All men lie and cheat."

"Women only want guys with money."

"I lost the love of my life and I'll never find love like that again."

"I am beginning to believe I will be alone for the rest of my life."

"I don't think there is someone for me in this city."

"I always pick the wrong type of person."

"To be in a relationship with someone, I need to give up a part of myself."

Our clients express these disempowering beliefs to us as if they are facts. Yet, in reality, they are the doubts and fears that have been allowed to take root. Doubts and fears can settle in your mind, become fixed, and are then part of your belief system. Whether the doubts or fears come from within, are given to you by someone else, or are a product of past pain, when you accept and internalize them, they become disempowering beliefs, and have power in your life. Sometimes these are irrational doubts and fears; sometimes they are based upon real experiences. Whichever is the case, if your beliefs are undermining your goals, you need to address them.

Allow yourself to experience your doubts and fears without holding onto them or faulting yourself for having them. Everyone has doubts and fears about themselves and the future. And again, we want to stress that doubts and fears are *not* your enemy. Learn to distinguish doubts and fears for what they are: thoughts and feelings, *not* the truth about your future. When you distinguish your fears from the truth, you will protect yourself from creating new disempowering beliefs.

Simon – The Unending Quest

To clearly illustrate the power of negative beliefs, we want to share the story of a former client whose disempowering beliefs stood between him and his happily ever after. His name was Simon. He was 6'2", gym fit, and extremely handsome. He worked as a stockbroker and enjoyed an affluent lifestyle. As if that wasn't enough, he was also outgoing and witty. He was easy to talk to and was one of those people who seemed to ooze charisma and self-confidence. He was, for all intents and purposes, a living embodiment of Disney's Prince Charming. On paper, he was the kind of man a matchmaker would dream of.

Simon was particular about everything in his life, from his clothes, to his car, and everything in between. The criteria for his partner was no exception. He wanted to meet a tall, attractive, blonde, strong-willed woman, who wasn't afraid to take charge and could match his demanding lifestyle. In short, a modern day Disney princess. A tall order, yes, but then, he was the "total package" himself.

Despite the specificity of his request, we were able to introduce him to several great candidates. The dates went well, but nothing stuck. Regardless, we continued to find women for him. It wasn't hard, since he was many women's dream date. We set him up with former models. We set him up with beautiful executives. We set him up with every tall, gorgeous, captivating blonde we could find, all to no avail. After working with him for several months, we started to hear the same response when we approached potential dates. "Simon? The tall guy? The stockbroker? Thanks, but no thanks."

What was going on? Until then, women had been beating down our door to go on a date with our Prince Charming. Unfazed, we continued with our search. Before long, though, we couldn't deny it: something was not right. Almost every time we suggested Simon to a woman, she would decline the date. It seemed like every woman who fit his requirements had already been on a date with him. Either that, or one of her friends had dated him. It turned out that his overactive online dating, happy-hour hopping, and our matchmaking efforts had resulted in Simon having met seemingly every tall single blonde in the city. And we live in a *big* city.

By this point, he probably had only one degree of separation from any single woman in town. He had developed a reputation. He wasn't a womanizer. That wasn't the issue. He was always courteous and respectful. Simon had developed a reputation as a "time-waster" and someone who wasn't *serious*. We knew this wasn't his intention. We knew just how seriously he was taking his search for love, just as we knew how important his time was to him. We spoke to Simon about what was going on, and he admitted to us that he had dated so many women that the process had turned into an unfulfilling blur. As he talked, we realized he had created such an idealized version of what he wanted that he was no longer searching for a real person, but an image of perfection. And as everyone knows, when it comes to human beings, no one is perfect. Simon instantly measured every woman he met against the perfect creature he had imagined, and, of course, they all fell short. Nobody was special, nobody would do, nobody could even come close. In his mind, he was doing everything he could to find the right woman. But deep down, he had lost hope.

He began to have doubts and feared that he would never find her. The longer he held onto his doubts and fears, the stronger they got. Eventually, he concluded that she didn't even exist in our city, and it became his truth. There was nothing we could do. Simon's disempowering belief that the right woman for him didn't exist in our city undermined all our efforts and became his reality. How could he ever find what he wanted if, in his heart, he didn't believe it existed? In this respect, he was a time-waster, but it was his own time he wasted the most. He was chasing the impossible. If you believe that something can never happen, the door is already closed, and no amount of banging will open it.

Again, it is vital to understand that doubts and fears can settle into your mind, become fixed, and become incorporated into your belief system. If you harbor a disempowering belief about yourself and your chances in dating, it can negate your efforts and become a self-fulfilling prophecy. Approach dating with optimism and faith, and that will make the difference.

Know Thyself

As matchmakers, we know that if a client doesn't believe they will find love and a fulfilling relationship, they won't. Until we help them overcome their disempowering belief, any other work we do for them will be in vain.

You may think that what you believe is out of your hands, that it's a done deal, set in stone— but this is not true. We all have the ability to change what we believe. First, you need to understand what you believe, and in order to do that, you need to look within.

People have always looked outside of themselves for signs about their future and ways to control life's events. What they don't understand is that their own beliefs are the greatest predictor of what is to come. The ancient Greeks went to the Temple of Apollo to consult the Oracle about their futures. Above the temple's entrance was the famous maxim: *Know Thyself*. Basically, this was written as a reminder for those who visited the Oracle that the only true way to see your own future, is to understand what you believe.

To *know thyself* means to be honest about your own beliefs. If you look inside yourself and find that your beliefs are not in accord with your desired future, what do you do? If your beliefs don't support your goals, look at how you can transform your beliefs. Change your beliefs, and in doing so, you will influence your future.

So, how can you change your beliefs?

Deconstructing Disempowering Beliefs

Take a good look at your disempowering beliefs and determine where they come from. Are they even your beliefs? Have they been given to you by someone else? Have they, like Tessa's, been passed down from your family or culture? It is very difficult to escape a mindset that has been ingrained since childhood, but it can be done.

Perhaps you developed your disempowering beliefs at a time in your life when your situation was different. They may come from a period when you were under a great deal of stress or in the aftermath of a painful loss: the death of a parent, the complicated end of a long-term relationship, or being laid off or fired from a job. When you form beliefs under such circumstances, they become reinforced by the emotions of that situation and can seem like essential truths about yourself or the world. You may decide that you are alone in the world, that you will always end up getting hurt, or that you are a failure. However, these beliefs only reflect your experience at that stressful or painful moment. These disempowering beliefs are neither truths about you, nor your future. Ask yourself: Do these beliefs still ring true? Do you still need them? Can you let them go? A hurt from the past may leave a mental scar. In such cases, it is vital to know: you now have the wisdom and personal power you did not possess when you were hurt.

Every major event in our lives will change us in some way; make sure that you direct that change for the better. Anything you have survived or overcome adds strength to your character. Don't try to bury something that shames you or hurts you; face it, take possession of it, and master it.

If you are unable to determine where your disempowering beliefs have come from, or feel you just aren't strong enough to confront them, consider consulting with a professional who can help you work through them. Your mind is like a garden. Pull up the weeds and plant what you want to grow. If something is too deeply rooted, or just too big for you to shift on your own, seek help. There are many ways to do this, and there are many highly qualified professionals who can help you. Only by dealing with your disempowering beliefs will you be ready to move forward.

Cultivating Positive Beliefs

Identifying and deconstructing disempowering beliefs clears the way for you to begin building a new and empowering belief system. The next step in creating a sound foundation for finding love is to begin cultivating positive beliefs. Like a disempowering belief, a positive belief is a truth, that *you create* for yourself and hold on to. However, a positive belief works to encourage and fortify your goals. Rather than being rooted in our doubts, fears, and past pain, positive beliefs come from our hopes, dreams, and loving and supportive life experiences.

There are many ways to cultivate positive beliefs and to anchor them in your consciousness. Through using supportive tools and taking daily steps, you can uplift yourself and your mindset about dating and the future. Some examples include: uplifting music, prayer, affirmations, guided meditation, vision boards, dancing, being social with positive people, keeping a gratitude journal, staying present to the good things in your life, reading books that inspire you, listening to positive podcasts, and attending personal development seminars.

Positive and empowering beliefs take more work to create than negative or disempowering ones. Have you ever wondered why you can remember a critical remark years after it was made, while the compliment you got ten minutes ago is already forgotten? As humans, we are hardwired to notice, learn from, and protect ourselves from things that might cause us pain or harm. Therefore, our negative experiences automatically have a more powerful impact on us. As a result, we must work harder to hold on to the good thoughts and establish them as personal truths. This is why we need to document, concentrate on, and celebrate positive experiences. Emphasizing positive and uplifting experiences gives you the power to create beliefs that will bring you closer to your desired future and your goal of love and a fulfilling relationship.

Keep in mind that the people around you will have a major impact on how you feel and the beliefs you carry. Whenever possible, surround yourself with friends and confidants who have a positive outlook on dating and relationships. Work with your friends to create a nurturing environment for dating. If you spend time with a friend who is jaded about romance or the chance of finding love, make sure their sentiments do not infect your own. The natural ups and downs of dating will mean that you will need encouragement. Nurture a strong belief in yourself, and make sure your social circle supports you in your search for love.

Keep your goal at the forefront of your mind. Tell yourself that you *can* have love in your life and that you *will* achieve it. Remember, we are not talking about just saying positive things that you may (or may not) believe. You need to approach life with a constructive and empowered mindset. That mindset will be reflected in your daily experiences. Living from a positive and empowered perspective will impact your actions and create your results.

Beliefs are powerful. A strong Belief has the power to make or break. A positive belief— a healthy, strong, empowering belief in yourself— can help you realize anything you put your mind to.

Believe!

ARE YOU REALLY OPEN TO LOVE? THE OPEN PREDICTOR

ARE YOU REALLY OPEN TO LOVE?
THE OPEN PREDICTOR

"The doors we open and close each day decide the lives we live."

–Flora Whittemore

NOTHING CAN enter through a closed door and nothing can be seen with closed eyes.

You need to be open to allow love to enter your life. This may seem like an obvious statement, but think about it for a minute. What does it mean to be open? How are you open to love, and, just as importantly, in what ways are you closed to love?

The Open Predictor is a broad concept that covers many issues: finding love in unexpected packages, notions of compromise, missed chances, the dangers of being too specific, distinguishing true desires from limiting criteria, and more. We will look at each of these topics in detail, but to begin, let's explore a common error in the dating world.

Be Inclusive, Not Exclusive

When people aren't successful in their search for love, they often tell us, "I'm just not being picky enough." Impatient with their progress, they narrow the criteria of who they are open to meeting. This choice is usually made out of frustration and as an attempt to take control of their search. They say, "I need to be more specific— that way I can stop wasting my time and get to the right candidates." Reducing your criteria is a common error and a bad move. It is the opposite of what you need to do. What if you were looking for something other than a life partner? How would you conduct your search? If you had lost your keys and hadn't found them after looking through the house, would it make sense to narrow your search to just the hallway and kitchen? Wouldn't it be more effective to look in every room, add a check of coat pockets, and even expand your search to the garage? So why do people insist on narrowing their search when it comes to looking for their match? They don't realize that, by reducing their criteria, they are actually limiting their chances of finding love.

It is critically important to recognize that the approach of narrowing your search is counterproductive. Avoid falling into its trap. Resist the impulse to limit your criteria, and adopt The Open Predictor. Be more open to the kinds of people you will meet. Be open to the possibility of finding love in unexpected ways, places, and packages. Love is an unfettered force; it can't be pinned down, confined within a labeled box, or constrained by a rigid list of qualities.

The more you limit your ideas of what form love will take, the less chance you will have of recognizing it when it tries to find you. Being too specific not only limits your options, it also limits your ability to see that someone might be a wonderful match for you. Reducing your criteria is like trying to appreciate a work of art by looking at it through a microscope. Stand back, widen your field of vision, and take in the bigger picture. Similarly, when it comes to a person, too much close attention to the small details will hinder your ability to see the person as a whole. Yes, there may be *one* thing about someone that isn't ideal, but overall that person may be just who you are looking for. If you can see beyond one deficit, you may be surprised to find countless merits.

Beyond Type

We all have our "types," meaning the material characteristics we say we find attractive.

"I like men with broad shoulders."

"I like women with dark hair."

"I like men who are clean-shaven."

"I like women who are shorter than me."

Ask anyone and they will provide you with "the list" of features they expect to find in their fantasy partner.

As matchmakers, we are used to people coming to us with "the list" of criteria in hand. They expect us to simply read the list, consult our database of potential dates, and, like a computer program, make a match. If only it were that simple! We are continually amazed by how common the Burger King "have it your way" approach to dating has become. We regularly meet people who have the attitude that finding a partner should be as simple as ordering a burger from a fast food menu. They want to be able to pick and choose from a list of specific traits and then have the exact combination handed to them in a convenient to-go bag. "Yeah, I'd like a tall man, wealthy, plenty of charm, extra laughs, and hold the kids. And I'll have that to go." Would you like fries with that life partner?

There is nothing wrong with having specific criteria that you value in a partner, and it's important to know the attributes that are crucial to your future relationship. However, believing that you can select an exact combination of traits and find it in another human being is unreasonable. If that person actually does exist, what are the odds that you will both be attracted to each other and compatible for a long-term relationship? Love doesn't work that way. Love is about being open to meeting many wonderful people and then discovering who you feel connected to and who you can build a good life with. Love can't be ordered up from a drive-thru menu. Love just doesn't work that way, and therefore, *we* can't work that way. We don't limit ourselves to the list. We look beyond it, because that's where love is found.

Beyond the List

Frequently, a client's list of criteria tells us more about their previous relationships than the one they truly hope to find. A list is often based on the pain a person encountered in past relationships. When they create their list, they choose criteria that is opposite to what caused their past pain. For example, if you are seeking a partner who is outgoing, you may be trying to compensate for a dissatisfying relationship with someone who was shy and not social. If you have an extreme emphasis on finding someone loyal, it's likely that you have been cheated on in the past. Seeking someone who is very adventuresome? Maybe your previous partner lacked spontaneity.

When we are presented with a list, the question we ask about every criterion is, "Why?" Why are you specifically looking for this trait? What made you want to find someone who explicitly displays this criteria? More often than not, the items on your list reflect what you don't want, or what you fear, rather than what you do want. Herein lies the fundamental error. Looking for love should not be about rebounding from this or that kind of person. Just because a relationship failed, does not mean that you need to overcorrect by looking for opposite qualities in the future. Humans are more than the sum of their parts.

Another major mistake people make when compiling their list is confusing one attribute with another. Some people confuse *what* someone does or has with *who* they are as a person and the content of their character. A new client may tell us, "I'm looking for someone with a college degree." When we ask why, the client responds by saying, "I want someone who is intelligent and successful." The error is in thinking that a college degree will ensure intellect and a good career, while the lack of a degree means someone is unintelligent and unsuccessful. Is this the case? Of course not. Another client may say, "I want to meet someone who is considerably younger," when what the client really means is that they want to be with someone who is active and has lots of energy. A client who desires financial security may ask to meet someone who has a well-paid job. Sorry to burst any bubbles with this one, but just because somebody has a high income does not mean they are financially responsible and secure. They could make more money than most, but still live paycheck to paycheck. These clients fail to realize that these criteria do not equate with character. "I'm looking for a high-powered businessman. I'm looking for a yoga instructor. I'm looking for . . . etc., etc." These clients mistakenly believe that a person who has the criteria they desire, or who does what they admire, will make them happy. Generally, when you prioritize *who* your potential partner is over *what* your potential partner has or does, you will be more successful in finding what you are looking for. To illustrate this point, let's look at the story of Amy and David.

Amy and David – The Curse of Criteria

Amy had been married to an irresponsible alcoholic. She had spent years as the sole breadwinner, raising the kids, keeping the home clean, and mothering her husband as well as the children. It was exhausting. Finally, enough was enough, and she divorced her husband. It broke her heart, but she knew she was making the right decision.

After a few years, she decided it was time to try again, and she came to us for help. Amy wanted love again, but this time, she was determined to find her true partner in life. She wanted someone who would help her carry the load. This was pretty much her only requirement, and after learning about her experience, we wanted that for her, too.

We had a great match for Amy. His name was David, and we told her all about him. He had a good job and enjoyed his work. He came from a loving family. He was nice-looking, easy-going, and an all-round decent guy. Interested and cautious, Amy listened intently.

"Sounds great!" said Amy, smiling. "How old is he?"

We told her. The smile vanished. "Oh. Oh, well, that's not going work for me. No, I don't think he's right. Who else do you have?"

Surprised, we asked about her sudden lack of interest. She explained to us that it was because David was five years younger than her. We didn't understand— sure, it's more common for a woman to be younger than the man, but five years? It wasn't that much of a difference. With a little coaxing, the truth came out. Amy felt that to be in a relationship with a younger man would be a repeat of her previous experience. She equated being younger with being irresponsible. It was only a five-year difference, but in her mind it meant that she would, once again, be shouldering the responsibility.

Again, Amy asked, "Who else do you have?"

Susie said, "I have plenty of other men, but you *must* meet *this* man!"

Susie insisted that David was great for Amy and that Amy needed to give him a chance. Begrudgingly, Amy agreed. She and David met for dinner and David's strong yet gentle demeanor won her over. She could see that he was mature and had built a good life. She relaxed and forgot all about the age difference. They had a wonderful evening together. After just a few hours, they felt more comfortable and connected than they had ever felt with anyone else.

Amy called first thing the next morning to tell us what a wonderful match David was for her. The funny thing was, Amy admitted to us, the only reason she had consented to the date was that she didn't want to anger her matchmakers! Amy and David eventually married. They share a wonderful life and their connection is obvious to everyone who sees them together.

There's more to this story than a happy ending. The fact is, had we stuck to Amy's rigid criteria and allowed it to dictate the men we matched her with, she never would have met David. Had we not persisted, *what* David was, his age, would have stood in the way of her discovering *who* David was— exactly the kind of man she was searching for.

Our years of experience have taught us that going against a list of criteria often brings great results. It took this conviction for us to get Amy and David together. It took effort for Amy to open herself up to the idea of dating a younger man. Insisting on a match like this can be quite a risk. We could have easily caused Amy to dig in her heels and become more rigid. However, we know that the opportunity to meet a truly compatible and wonderful person is rare and can be fleeting. We weren't going to let Amy miss this one. It does take being open to meet someone who doesn't match your list— but you just may find the love of your life.

When we tell you to look outside your list, we want you to be more open. We don't want you to compromise the essential criteria that reflects your values and life goals. If you are devout in your faith and wish to share your belief in God with a partner, we wouldn't suggest that you meet an atheist. If you want to start a family, we wouldn't recommend that you meet people who don't share that desire. Where Amy and David were concerned, we understood Amy's reasoning for not wanting a younger man, yet we knew that in this case, his age was not in conflict with her values and emotional needs.

We want to emphasize that it is entirely acceptable to stick to the kind of deal breakers that protect you from an unhealthy or unfulfilling relationship. However, being too specific with your criteria will be counterproductive to finding love. When you make your list, and we know you will, take your time. Don't worry about being efficient. Examine each item on your list. Ask yourself, "Does this trait express what I really want?" Make sure that the items you are listing won't exclude the right person. There is nothing wrong with having some criteria, as long as it doesn't undermine your search.

Why do we rely on our lists? As we noted earlier, it is often a way to try to take control of the search process, or to protect yourself from repeating past mistakes. Yet another reason people use lists has to do with convenience. To a certain degree, relying on criteria is a form of laziness. It's like trying to take a shortcut. It's a way of trying to save time and avoid the hard work of separating the candidates with potential from the masses. Finding and evaluating potential matches takes a lot of time. Believe us, we know. We have decades of experience searching for people, uncovering who they are and understanding their values and goals— it's what we do every day. There is no shortcut for meeting people in person and actually talking with them. You can't run a very specific list through a computer and come up with the perfect life partner. It might seem efficient, and yes, you may meet people who conform to your criteria, but that doesn't mean that they are right for you. What's more, you will miss out on wonderful people who don't exactly fit your specifications, one of whom might be the love of your life. If you open yourself to unimagined possibilities, unimaginable happiness can come your way.

Unexpected Treasure

So often, love is an unexpected treasure. As John Barrymore once said, "Happiness often sneaks in through a door you didn't know you left open." Most people have never considered the fact that each criterion on their list eliminates thousands of potential partners. Of course, the very reason for having criteria is to help you narrow your search in the hope that you will find the right person. But being too specific in your search for just about anything in life can cause you to miss out on something new, wonderful, and unexpected.

Imagine you are online, looking for a new place to eat. You want the food to be delicious, the service to be great, and the atmosphere to be warm and inviting. You go to an online restaurant guide and begin clicking on your desired features. You select your price range, star rating, and open for dinner. But then you keep going. You click takes reservations, outdoor dining, has live music, and you narrow the search area to a two-mile radius. You submit your search and end up with a list of the same 10 restaurants you've been going to for years. What you don't know is that you've eliminated this wonderful little spot that's just a couple neighborhoods away and is topping the list of all the restaurant review columns. Having some criteria is helpful when conducting an online search for the perfect place to eat. But even in looking for a new restaurant, checking too many boxes can eliminate a great option and keep you in your same old rut. If it doesn't work when you're looking for a new place to eat, then love certainly isn't something that corresponds with checkboxes. Love isn't about efficiency and convenience. Love is expansive. Love is a great big YES to the world! The search for love should be as wide and open as possible.

Dan and Jessica – Oh that List

Dan was a really great guy. He was handsome, outgoing, charismatic, polite, and sincere. And he was funny! The first time he met with us, he had us laughing, almost non-stop, for two hours. It's a wonder we got anything done at all. In between the laughs, we managed to get down to the details.

After saying our goodbyes, we quickly brainstormed about who should be his first date. We thought of Jessica right away and knew that Dan would like her. She was a cute, bubbly redhead whose carefree and easygoing manner was natural and irresistible. She lived for the moment. She was a professional who had never had kids, and she felt that her life was full and complete without them. She whirled into our offices like a tiny tornado of smiles and goodwill. Jessica lived downtown in a neat little condo that was as bright and cheerful as she was. She was a happy person, delighted with life, and wanted someone like herself to share it with.

Jessica had been divorced for several years and had taken on dating like a part-time job. She was enjoying herself and enjoying the process, yet she wasn't getting the results she wanted. By the time she came to us, she believed she had it all figured out. She had analyzed her mistakes and come to the conclusion, as so many do, that she wasn't being specific enough about what she wanted. She explained to us that, although she'd had fun, she clearly needed to narrow her criteria and only date men whose qualities matched what she "knew" her future partner needed to have. She'd decided she needed to find someone who lived in the city, was a college-educated professional, and had no children at home.

We knew that Dan would be perfect for Jessica. In terms of their sense of humor and enthusiasm for life, Dan and Jessica were two peas in a pod. But there was a catch. Dan did not fit her increasingly restrictive criteria. On paper, their specific qualities were not a match. Yet we knew that, in person, they would instantly click. We were sure they would get along wonderfully, if, and only if, Jessica could see past her list. We just had to figure out how to make it happen. Susie didn't hesitate, she picked up the phone and called Jessica.

"Hello? Jessica? Hi, it's Susie. Listen, I've met your husband . . . Yes, your husband!" Caught a little off guard, Jessica asked for details. Susie began describing Dan: his charisma, his positive approach to life, and his hilarious sense of humor. Jessica was intrigued. Susie went on, painting an honest portrait of the man. However, she did leave a few details out, like the fact that Dan had not completed his college degree. She didn't mention that he was not a white collar professional and worked in a factory. She left out that he had two kids in high school and a co-parenting situation that was less than amicable. If that wasn't enough, there was also his location. Dan lived out of town and in the country. After years of living in the city, he'd decided he'd had enough. Wanting a more relaxed and less complicated lifestyle, he'd bought a small farmhouse and a fair amount of the surrounding land. Susie didn't mention any of it to Jessica. She just set up the date.

Hey, we know what you're thinking. Our tactics were underhanded. We didn't tell the whole truth. And how do we answer that charge? We plead guilty to all of it. Yep, we didn't tell the whole truth. Then again, we didn't lie! Susie did not make up any details or invent a single fact. As Irish statesman Edmund Burke would have put it, she merely exercised an economy of truth. We saw the bigger picture, and we knew they would connect instantly. Yet we also knew that if Jessica had all the information from the start, (his location, his kids, his job, his lack of college degree), she would have dismissed him immediately.

It was a risk, yes, just as it was a risk for us to pester Amy into going on a date with someone younger when it conflicted with her criteria. When you take a risk, you weigh the chance that you might lose something you value against the chance that you might gain something you value. For us, the risk was losing the trust of valued clients versus helping our clients find an amazing life partner. For Jessica, and for Amy before her, the risk was losing a few hours versus meeting the loves of their lives. In both cases, we carefully weighed the potential loss against the potential gain and came to the conclusion that the risk was warranted. Sometimes, risk is just what is needed.

Jessica and Dan went on a date.

Fingers crossed, all we could do now was wait to find out how the evening went.

The very next morning, at the office, Elizabeth took a call from Jessica. She told her to put it on speaker so she could speak to both of us. With nervous glances passing between us, our hearts pounding, we prepared for the worst.

"You guys!" she began. Her tone was somewhere between accusation and astonishment.

"Yes?"

"I can't believe you two," said Jessica, almost shouting.

"So, uh, how was the date?"

"How was it? . . ." We heard her take a deep breath. "It was wonderful!"

Relief poured over us. "You had a good time?"

"A good time?" repeated Jessica. "I haven't laughed that much since I was sixteen years old. We had so much fun. We ate so much food and talked all evening. Then we went to a bar and kept on talking and laughing!"

"So, everything's good . . . did Dan talk about himself much?" Susie asked.

"We talked about everything. And yeah, he told me where he lives. And yeah, about his kids, and ex-wife, education, and what he does. And you know what? I don't care about any of it. I'm just happy to have met such a great guy who I can have so much fun with."

They met again, and within two weeks they were dating regularly. Lunch dates, dinner dates, telephone calls. We left them to their own devices, hoping, for both their sakes, that something would come of their relationship.

It did. They got married about two years after we introduced them. Believe it or not, Jessica sold her condo and moved out to the sticks. We caught up with her recently, and she entertained us with stories of life in the countryside. Having been a city girl all her life, she was discovering all the beauty of nature. They kept bees, harvested the honey fresh from the hives, and shared it with their friends in the city. Rural living agreed with her. The fact that Dan had children was also a source of happiness for her. The kids may have been on their way to independence, but Jessica was learning the joy of helping someone find their feet, and the pride of seeing a person you care about emerge as an autonomous human being. Dan went on to finish his college degree. They have a great life together.

Quite often it's best not to know too much about someone before you meet them. Sometimes, the experience of discovering who a person really is allows love to develop. On paper, Jessica and Dan were not suited. In person, they were drawn to each other magnetically, and they found a once-in-a-lifetime love.

Many people want to believe that if they meet someone who has every characteristic on their list, they will fall in love. But we don't fall in love with who someone is on paper, or in a profile, or from what we can discern from a list of criteria. Falling in love depends on who you actually are in the real world: the living, breathing, smiling, crying, fragile, courageous, *open* you. Even if you know a person's list of characteristics and accomplishments, until you meet them and spend time with them, you don't, and can't, know who they truly are. You fall in love as you *discover* the other person: their values, their character, their good points, their shortcomings, and their reactions as they discover the same things about you. In this respect, love is a journey, not an event. In this journey, you have to let things unfold. Not everything will be under your control, but this is a good thing— this is what allows for the unexpected attractions, unforeseen connections, and new adventures.

Dr. Jacks and Dr. Max – Control Versus Adventure

Within the space of two days, we interviewed two doctors. Dr. Jacks and Dr. Max were in their mid 40s, rather average-looking, and almost nerdy. Professionally, they were both very successful, widely recognized, and highly esteemed in their respective fields. Despite all of their similarities, they had two distinctly different approaches to finding their matches. Dr. Jacks had a very detailed list of qualifications for the woman he wanted to meet. She had to be younger than 40, super intelligent, successful in her career, athletic, with no children and no interest whatsoever in having them in the future. And as for how she looked, he said, "On a scale of one to ten, she has to be no less than a nine and preferably a blonde."

Dr. Max came to us with a completely different plan. When we asked him about the kind of woman he would like to meet, he said simply, "I will meet ANYONE who wants to meet me." "Anyone?" we asked, surprised. "Yes. Anyone." This was something that we had never heard before. This wasn't even an approach that we would have recommended to our clients. But we were intrigued and interested in seeing where this experiment would go.

Dr. Jacks's approach, though extreme, was more familiar to us, and in spite of his incredibly narrow range of qualifications, we thought we had the perfect match. Abigail was 39 years old, exceptionally attractive, blonde, smart, and a professional. She had no children and had given up on having them. Just what the doctor ordered. We would have been hard pressed to find a woman who could better meet his limiting list. We sent them out on their first date. It went well. In fact, it went so well that they started to see each other regularly. Their personalities and lifestyles complimented each other in many ways, and in no time at all, they were enjoying a great relationship.

About a year later, they were out having a lovely lunch on a patio when a woman pushing a stroller stopped next to them. Abigail couldn't help but notice how adorable the baby was. Smiling, she turned to Dr. Jacks and commented on how nice it must be to be a mother. Dr. Jacks made some vague noise and asked if she wanted dessert.

A few days later, Abigail was on her way to an out-of-town conference. When she checked her voicemail, she was surprised to hear a message from Dr. Jacks saying that it was over, and he would drop her things off at her house. Just like that.

Let's go back to Dr. Max. He was having a great time with the dating process. He was meeting all types of women and thoroughly enjoying himself on every date. He told us, "Before every date, I ask myself one question: what can I give to this experience?" Dr. Max never looked at dating as a waste of his time. He saw the process as an adventure that was full of life changing opportunities. It was a wonderful approach, and he reaped its rewards. Of all the women Dr. Max met that year, there were two who truly changed the course of his life. One had a substantial impact on his career by co-authoring an acclaimed article that was published in a prestigious medical journal. The other helped him change his style from nerdy and easily overlooked to sophisticated and memorable. Both women helped him grow to become the confident man who was ready to meet the love of his life. Dr. Max's experiment worked. In the end, he met his amazing match, and they are very happy together.

And Dr. Jacks? Who knows. Whether or not he will ever find his match is yet to be determined.

The stories of our two doctors emphasizes how being open will significantly improve your likelihood of dating success. Dr. Jacks was so specific about what he wanted that he ended up looking for someone who has probably never even existed. He was searching for a fantasy. On the other hand, Dr. Max was completely open to whatever might happen. Rather than fixating on the end result, he enjoyed the process, made wonderful friends and business connections, grew as a person, and ended up meeting the love of his life. Dr. Max's experiment shows us that if you are open, each time you go on a date, you can gain some new knowledge about about yourself, about another human being, or about the world around you.

Don't Settle

Now, you are probably wondering what happened to Abigail. She had always been open about the kind of men she would meet, which was a good thing, but she made one big mistake. Abigail confused being open with settling.

After hearing Dr. Jacks's voicemail, she called our office and told us what happened. Over the course of a long conversation, her true desires came to light. Long before we had even met her, Abigail had given up on the life she truly wanted. Knowing that her age likely precluded her from having children, she was willing to settle for what she considered to be the next best thing. She threw herself into her career and became open to men, like Dr. Jacks, who could give her companionship and compliment her current lifestyle, but couldn't give her the life and family she really wanted. We made a pact with her that we would upgrade her dreams. Abigail quickly regrouped, and we all got to work making her dreams come true.

It was not long before a charming police officer found his way into our office. He wanted all the things that Abigail wanted, a loving home, someone to share his life with, and the opportunity to have children. Abigail was the first and only woman we called. Today, Abigail is a wife and the mother of two beautiful boys. She quit her corporate job and is now a stay at home mom doing what she loves to do best.

Like Abigail, sometimes people confuse the concept of being open with settling on their dreams. Other times people think that being open is equivalent to settling for less in a life partner. We want you to have love, connection, and happiness, but know that those things may not show up in the package you imagine. We once had a woman say, "I won't go out with him, he's bald, I just won't settle." Finding love with someone who has less hair than you imagined is not settling.

What is settling? Settling is being with someone who: you aren't attracted to; you don't truly love; doesn't share your values; doesn't support your goals and dreams; isn't someone you can trust; isn't kind to you; or hurts you. Settling is being with someone whom you can't have a happy life with. Being open to a wider field of potential partners is *not* synonymous with lowering your standards, giving up your dreams, or settling.

Let's think about Jessica and Dan. He didn't live in the city, he had children, and he didn't have the career she expected. In more ways than not, Dan didn't match Jessica's criteria. Do you think Jessica settled? We know for a fact that Jessica doesn't believe that she settled in any way. Jessica knows that she married an amazing man and the love of her life. And she is happier now than she ever could have imagined. When we suggest that you be open, we don't mean downgrading or settling for less! Understanding this concept is a vital part of The Open Predictor.

We were once at a dinner party with a large group of friends. It was late in the evening, the wine was flowing, and everyone's inhibitions had fallen away when the conversation turned to love and the search for a partner. One man said, "Finding love always demands a compromise." His opinion was that love was impossible without settling on some level. Hearing his statement, another guest, who had been quietly listening for most of the discussion, piped up and said, "Love is not a compromise if what you end up with is greater than what you could have imagined." The room fell quiet for a moment as each of us considered her statement. How can love, the richest and most fulfilling activity a human can engage in, be equated with concession?

Opening the Door to Love

We ask our clients to be as open as possible about who they will meet. This doesn't mean that we think they should sacrifice attraction, compatibility, and romance to get into a relationship. We want you to invite love into your life by opening the door. Don't just crack it open— love may not make it through. Instead, open it wide. Throw the door open as wide as possible and welcome love into your life! Now isn't the time to be picky. Now is the time to maximize your choices. Meet a variety of people, gain a greater understanding of what you truly want in a relationship, and clear up misconceptions about what you thought you wanted. The time to be picky is when you ultimately choose whom to spend your life with. Pick someone wonderful whom you are attracted to, completely in love with, and with whom you can share a happy life. Being open has nothing to do with settling. NEVER settle, ALWAYS be open.

Begin by considering your list of qualifications for your potential partner. Think about everything on that list and understand where it comes from. Have you included a trait that says more about a previous relationship than the one you hope to begin? Is your list so limiting that you will have very few options? Is it so narrow that you may have eliminated your potential match? Are you picky in a way that actually serves you, or does it keep you alone?

It is also important to ask yourself if your list is more concerned with *what* the person is, than *who* the person is. If so, rewrite your list so that it reflects the *who* instead of the *what*. Make these changes by asking yourself why you have chosen a specific qualification. For example: If your requirements specify someone with an advanced degree, ask yourself why. When we ask our clients this question, we often hear, "I am looking for someone educated so that we can have thoughtful conversations and meaningful discussions." Or, "I have an advanced degree and I don't want a partner who will feel intimidated." We help our clients to understand that who they are actually looking for is someone intelligent, informed, and who enjoys insightful conversations, or someone who has confidence in themselves and expertise in their chosen profession. Not only is this more open, it is also a much more accurate way to describe the kind of person they want. There are many people with advanced degrees who possess none of these qualities. Figuring out what you are really asking for when you make your list will not only help you widen your field of potential partners, but also be more accurate in your search.

If you are like most people, when you think about the kind of person you are open to meeting, you probably miss one major consideration. Turn the tables for a moment. Is the person your list is describing looking for someone like *you*? Remember, what the other person wants is half of the equation. Susie once had the experience of listening to a man reel off a long list of prerequisites, and then, as an afterthought, he added, "Oh, and she would have to like me."

Asking for interests and qualities that you do not have works against your chances of finding love. You need to lead a lifestyle that will resonate with someone you consider a potential partner. For instance, we have often heard people who are reserved and not very social say, "I want to meet someone outgoing and fun who will bring me out of my shell and help me enjoy life more." But we never hear people who are outgoing and fun say, "I want to meet a reserved person and help them open up." An outgoing person may be fine with dating someone who isn't the life of the party, but they are still looking for someone who compliments their lifestyle.

Once, we interviewed a man who loved fast food and had an aversion to exercise. He told us that he wanted to be with someone who had a lean, fit figure. We asked him, "Can you tell us why that kind of woman would be looking for you?" Never really answering our question, he explained that this was the kind of woman he was attracted to, and he wanted his partner to be a good influence on him and get him to the gym. We have found that people who value fitness and a healthy lifestyle want to meet someone who shares those values and is already living a life that is in accordance with them.

If the kind of person you want to meet has the characteristics *X, Y* and *Z,* and you don't possess *X, Y* and *Z,* realize you need to adjust your criteria or take steps to develop these characteristics in yourself. You need to be open to dating the kind of person who is open to dating you. Ask yourself, "Would the kind of person I want to date be interested in dating me?" If the answer is anything short of "absolutely," take the steps to move yourself in that direction.

When we meet with a potential client, we ask them to do a short exercise with us. We say to them, "Let's pretend I am your fairy godmother, and I can grant you three wishes for your potential partner, but just three. What are the three most important characteristics you want in your match?" With this exercise, we can get an idea of their mindset, who they are looking for, and what matters most to them.

Try this exercise yourself. If you could only ask for three attributes in your potential life partner, what would they be? Ask yourself; what are the three fundamental characteristics that will make someone compatible with you? In choosing only three, you obviously have to give up many others. Would you give up attractiveness for character? Would you give up wealth for kindness? If you were a woman who liked to date tall men, would you forego this preference for intelligence or loyalty? This simple exercise can help to weed out any superfluous demands or personality traits you had previously imagined to be vital. It's a powerful exercise in exploring what qualities matter most to you.

Being open doesn't end with who you decide to meet. Staying open is just as important. All too often, we watch people quickly cast aside someone after one uneventful date or even just one quick conversation— like Emma did with Alex, the first time she met him. Don't make quick judgments. One of our Matchmaker Secrets is to always plan to go on at least three dates with a candidate, even if you don't think there is a strong match. (There are exceptions to this secret, but they are strictly limited to people who make you feel unsafe, deeply offend you, make you feel uneasy, or misrepresent themselves.) There are a couple reasons for the three date secret. One important reason is that attraction does not always surface immediately. It can grow and reveal itself over time. For women, connections and attraction often increase as they spend time with a man and feel comfortable with him. For men, attraction is generally more immediate, but this doesn't mean that it can't be developed if given time. Remember that attraction can, and does, develop. Allow attributes to reveal themselves, and let your attraction grow.

Another reason behind the three date secret is that people are often nervous on first dates. They may act out of character. Some people will talk too much just to fill the awkward silences, while others become reserved and don't reveal enough about themselves for you to connect with them. There are any number of defenses that interfere with getting to see the real person. Be equally aware of your own defenses, and keep in mind that they may be standing in the way of a connection. Remember that you are both on a first date and try not to put too much pressure on your date or on yourself.

Many people interpret immediate chemistry as a sign that they are meant to be with a certain person. Similarly, they use lack of initial chemistry as a sign they are not meant to be with a certain person. Of course, we want you to be physically attracted, intellectually stimulated, and emotionally bonded with the person you choose as your life partner. But it is vital to keep in mind: chemistry can, and does develop; chemistry can, and does fade. Chemistry can occur with someone with whom we *cannot* build a happy life, and it is not a sign that someone is or isn't *right* for us. Chemistry is just one part of the connection we can have with a life partner. **Understand that *initial* chemistry, or the lack of it, is not the way to determine if someone is or isn't right for you.**

Some people have so many qualifications on their list that only a few people in the world could fulfill it. This is extremely limiting. We all have certain qualities or types of people we are usually attracted to. However, most people have, at one time or another, been attracted to someone who fell outside those parameters. We find that 50% of the time our clients end up falling in love with someone who is very different than what they imagined and does not meet the criteria on their original list. If you ask many happy couples if the life partner they chose is exactly the kind of person they expected to be with, at least half will say no and that their mate was a surprise to them.

Recently, we were explaining The Open Predictor to one of our clients, and toward the end of the discussion she asked us if we had ever worked with someone who was genuinely open and still failed to find a relationship. We thought long and hard, and in the end, we couldn't think of an example. All the people who have come to us for help, and have been truly open and stuck with the process, have found love.

Not everyone has a matchmaker— someone as bold as we are who will be insistent and not take no for an answer. Yet even when we intervene with our clients, it is up to them to open their hearts. Being open is something you need to do for yourself. You need to look within, let go of the limitations you have put on love, and advocate for your own happiness.

Open the door and invite love into your life!

THE UPS, THE DOWNS, AND FINDING BALANCE

THE BALANCE PREDICTOR

THE UPS, THE DOWNS, AND FINDING BALANCE
THE BALANCE PREDICTOR

When we have a good balance between thinking and feeling...
our actions and lives are always the richer for it.

–Yo-Yo Ma

THE BALANCE Predictor is the glue that holds all the other predictors together. Why is Balance so important in the search for love? The answer is quite simple: the dating process is a veritable roller coaster of emotions— in order to reach your goal, maintaining emotional balance is essential.

Dating is an endeavor where the stakes could not be higher: love, happiness, and the future. The dating journey has a particular destination in mind, but the route is constantly being recalculated, and the means of reaching the destination are often vague. The intent is finding love, but how you are going to fall in love and who it will be with are unclear. It is a journey we set out on knowing that literally anything could happen. With so much on the line, the process of dating can, and will, produce emotional extremes. We go from the low down despair of feeling that you will never find someone, to the dizzying heights of early romance and all the potential for happiness that it promises. We are talking the whole emotional gamut— the everything and nothing of the human heart.

For most people, love is what gives life meaning. Love is the greatest element of the crazy, mixed up mess that is being human. Is it any wonder that we invest so much time, energy, and emotion in the search? Emotion is to love what money is to finance. Emotion is the currency of love, and as we search for love, we often spend our emotions as if they are a limitless resource, but they are not. This is why the Balance Predictor is so important. It is balance that ensures we do not become emotionally bankrupt. By maintaining our balance, we are better able to manage our emotional resources so that we can see our search through to our goal.

We all know the lows and highs of dating. There is the profound exhaustion of coming home from yet another disappointing first date with the fear that you will *never* find love and the feeling that all is in vain. You feel as though you are standing at the base of an insurmountable wall, with no footholds and no rope to pull yourself up. It may be that the very next date you go on will be the one that changes everything. But down there, in the shadow of the wall, it seems there is little light to brighten your heart.

It could be that you are at the other end of the spectrum. You have just come home from the best date of your life. You laughed, you talked, you felt as though a real and precious connection had been made. At last, you have found someone who is right for you and you are just as right for them! You are standing on the very top of the wall, and from your vantage point, you imagine you can see your life spreading out before you like a dream come true. But it may be that you are only one telephone call away from having all of these hopes dashed. Perhaps your date wasn't that into you. Maybe you chose to ignore something about them that you knew, in your heart, would eventually spoil it all.

These are the highs and lows. These are the sunny peaks and the dark valleys of dating. In order to be able to negotiate the extremes— in order to be able to find a happy path, not too high where the air is thin and makes you dizzy, nor too low, where the light is weak and the going is hard— you need to keep perspective. Emotional balance allows you to look upon your situation with perspective. With perspective, you can see the good and the bad, the highs and the lows, and you can find your way between them.

Rachel – The Resilient

When Rachel came to us, she was clear about what she wanted: love, marriage, and a family. Rachel was smart and attractive with a caring nature. She was in her late thirties and had been divorced for a few years. She told us that her marriage had been an education, and the greatest lessons she had taken from it were a better understanding of the pain that love can produce and the danger of holding on, for too long, to a relationship that isn't right. Knowing she wanted her romantic future to be very different from her past, she initially came to us for coaching. She felt that she was always attracted to the wrong kind of men. Even if her relationships were good in the beginning, they eventually became draining and unfulfilling. She'd had enough and wanted to do something about it.

Elizabeth coached with her for a while and was happy to see that Rachel was the kind of person who could take straightforward advice. They began by developing Rachel's emotional balance and her perspective. With a little time, Elizabeth helped Rachel understand that, in her past relationships, she had been afraid to bring up important concerns. She believed that if she loved someone, then she should be able to get past her worries and make the relationship work. As a result, she would ignore her concerns and hope that things would get better on their own. For Rachel, when a serious relationship ended, she felt like a failure. Without balance and perspective, Rachel was stopped by her fear. She was afraid that if she talked about problems, she would create friction and destabilize her relationships.

Now, through working with Elizabeth, Rachel realized that this level of fear was disproportionate to the actual risk of bringing up a difficult subject— while talking about an issue could be uncomfortable, it was not likely to end a relationship. She came to see that discussing difficult issues when they came up was the only way to know if a relationship was healthy and had a future. Even if she was attracted to someone and felt a connection with them, she needed to step back and talk about concerns rather than sweep them under the rug. As she developed her emotional balance, she also came to understand that if she was emotionally invested in a relationship that wasn't working, she could end it without feeling like a failure.

After a few months, Rachel felt she was ready to get back into the dating world. She decided that, in addition to coaching with Elizabeth, she wanted us to be her matchmakers. On her first few dates, Rachel had fun and met some interesting men.

When we decided to introduce her to Jack, we were excited and had a feeling that it would be a great match. Their feedback couldn't have been more positive. They really hit it off. He was taken with this "smart and sexy" woman. She told us that he was "the trifecta: fun, intelligent, and handsome," and said, "He just might be The One." They had a lot in common and strong physical chemistry. Very quickly, they found themselves in a serious relationship.

Eventually, Rachel and Jack began to discuss their future. They talked about living together, about selling one of their houses, and about how they would decorate. Rachel was excited and looking forward to this new chapter in her life. However, she could tell that these conversations about the future were a little strained. Rachel worried that Jack was suffering from nerves and had begun to withdraw emotionally. With her newfound perspective, she examined the situation instead of ignoring her concerns. Determined to straighten things out, Rachel initiated a discussion. They were honest about their feelings, and he admitted to her that he was unsure and didn't feel he was ready for such a big step.

Following this conversation, the relationship stalled and eventually ended. Rachel felt heartbroken. Jack was also feeling hurt. He reached out to her, and soon they were back together. They found relief in being with each other and promised to make it work this time. However, it didn't take long for the subject of their future to come up again. In order for their relationship to develop, they needed to take the next step. Again, Jack was unsure.

Conscious that her patterns from the past could derail her present, she was determined to keep a level head. Rachel made the difficult decision to, once again, confront Jack about his uncertainty. She told him she needed to move on. Rachel ended the relationship again, this time for good.

Heartache. Pain. Despair. She felt it all. In spite of it, Rachel was able to see beyond her immediate feelings. With her perspective, she was able to experience the end of the relationship without believing that she would never have love in her life. She recognized her painful feelings as a part of the process. More importantly, she knew they wouldn't last. This awareness gave her flexibility. It gave her the ability to yield, but not collapse. Despite her pain, she could move forward.

Rachel bounced back, and made an appointment with us. When she returned to our office, she sat down in front of us and declared, "I'm hurting. My heart is broken for the second time, but I'm done mourning this relationship. It's time to start dating again. I want love in my life, and I will not just sit back and waste my chance for love and a family."

We began setting up introductions for Rachel, and after a few dates had come and gone, we asked her how she was doing. Rachel told us, "At first I was dreading dating again. Then I thought, if I'm going out for an evening, I'm going to make sure I enjoy it. And I did. I just let myself have some fun. I'm realizing how nice a date can be when you let go, enjoy the moment, and don't worry about where it could lead." It was clear to us that, through her relationship with Jack, she had gained even more perspective. She had learned not to fixate on the outcome of a date or try to rush into a new relationship.

Some weeks later, we interviewed a new client, Adam. He was unusually honest and direct. He told us he wasn't sure that we could help him. He said he didn't want to waste money, or time— his or ours. We explained our process, dispelled a few misconceptions, and offered him our encouragement. By the end of the conversation, he and Susie had formed a connection. He trusted her, and she could see great potential for him.

Once he left our office, Susie, barely able to contain herself, said, "That's Rachel's future husband."

"You think so?"

"I know so."

The date was arranged.

When she went on the date with Adam, Rachel had a good time. She was relaxed and able to treat the evening for what it was— a night out with a pleasant stranger. It surprised her just how much they had in common. At the end of the date, she realized that, for the first time in a long time, she was excited about the prospect of a second date. She later told us that, even though she felt these emotions stirring, she did not let them jump ahead of herself like she had in her relationship with Jack. She wanted love again, but she knew that she needed more than just a spark. Like she had done on the first date with Adam, Rachel reminded herself to enjoy the second date for exactly what it was— a couple of pleasant hours with a nice man, who was becoming less of a stranger.

They started to date regularly. In those early days, one difficult issue arose. A romantic and generous man, Adam started sending candy and flowers to Rachel at her office. Unfortunately, Adam was unaware of how private a person Rachel was and that his gestures were making her uncomfortable. It was an innocent mistake, but it was one that made Rachel feel uneasy. She felt it was too soon for him to be making such romantic gestures and for her entire office to know about him. She liked her co-workers, but she didn't share details about her personal life with them. Since she had never talked about anyone she dated with them, they assumed things with Adam must be very serious and began asking questions. It was a new relationship, and she didn't have the answers. Still unsure of how she felt about Adam, Rachel worried that all of these gifts might be a sign that he was falling too fast.

At first, Rachel was overwhelmed. His actions seemed pushy and inconsiderate, and her initial reaction was to just break up with him. However, her perspective allowed her to pause and consider the situation from another possible point of view. From everything else she knew about Adam, he seemed like a great guy, and just maybe, this might be a misunderstanding. She would never know if she didn't talk to him. Though she didn't want to seem ungrateful or rude, she knew she had to broach the subject.

Adam was surprised. In an instant, he saw how much this subject troubled her and immediately explained himself, dispelling her fears. Adam was raised in a family where thoughtfulness was expressed through gift giving. He even sent his matchmakers chocolates and wine to say thank you for their help. Adam knew how hard Rachel worked, and his intention was to let her know he was thinking of her and to brighten her day. He told her, "I love giving gifts to people I like. And I do like you, but I agree it's definitely too soon for anyone to be under the impression that we are already in a serious relationship." He quickly apologized and promised all future gifts would be delivered to her privately. After their open conversation, Rachel's anxiety melted away. Soon, they did become serious, and the episode became one of those funny stories from early dating that they laugh about.

Within 18 months, they were married, and Rachel became a loving stepmother to Adam's four-year-old daughter. They bought a home and continue to build a wonderful life together.

None of Rachel and Adam's happiness could have happened if Rachel had not been able to achieve perspective. Each time Rachel came to a difficult juncture in her dating life, her emotional balance allowed her to move forward in a positive and constructive manner:

—When she found herself in a failing relationship, she was able to pull herself out and move forward. She was able to go back to dating without taking a long break and without blaming herself, or anyone else, for the breakdown of the relationship.

—When she met Adam, she was able to let the relationship develop and let his character emerge in its own time. She didn't let fears of the past or fantasies of the future prevent her from staying focused on what was happening in the present.

—When Adam's actions made her uncomfortable early in the relationship, she was able to discuss and work through her concerns with him, instead of ignoring it or just walking away.

Rachel's emotional balance gave her the perspective she needed to weather the ups and downs of her search for a loving life partner. Her emotional balance allowed her to stick with the process until she found what she was looking for. Dating is one of the few areas in our lives where we fail over and over again and still continue to try. Success is dependent on our ability to pick ourselves up, brush ourselves off, and go at it again. With emotional balance and the perspective it brings, you can avoid falling victim to the emotional extremes that are inherent in dating. Without emotional balance, a bad date or two can easily turn into a six month break from dating. This is vital: emotional balance allows us to keep going and to stay in the process as long as it takes. Emotional balance gives you the endurance and staying power you need. If you don't have a matchmaker, it's up to you to push yourself. You have to motivate yourself. Too often we hear:

"I can't take this."

"This is just too exhausting."

"I need a break."

"I'm giving up."

But we know that, if you take too much time off from dating, you can miss your chance. Believe us, we understand just how much work goes into finding a match and the entire dating process. As we said in the last chapter, finding love is a journey, not an event. It takes resolve and resilience. With emotional balance, you can avoid the pitfalls of expecting love to show up on the first date or starting to believe that you will never succeed.

Without a sense of perspective, without emotional balance, you will become little more than a rag doll, swinging from high to low, from anxiety to confidence, from happiness to despair. A centered perspective is the vantage point from where you can observe the ups and downs of dating. From that place, you can avoid becoming a slave to your emotions and sabotaging your chance of finding love.

Enjoying Dating

We want you to find love and we want you to enjoy the process. In fact, enjoying the dating process is critical to your success. Merely surviving it or just going through the motions will have a detrimental effect on your results. Looking for a partner does not have to be a relentless slog. It should be a worthwhile experience in its own right. Whether you are at an event, working on your online dating profile, or out with a date, focus on enjoying each moment rather than fixating on the end goal of finding "The One." Don't forget it completely— just allow your immediate situation to take precedence.

Like Rachel did when she met Adam, keep in mind how nice a date can be when you enjoy the present moment rather than worry about where it could lead. When you meet someone for the first time, try not to instantly compare them to your fantasies or fears. Do your best to make every date a positive experience for *both* of you. You will be invited to talk about yourself, your goals, your best memories, and your cherished visions of the future. You will have the honor of listening to someone else share these parts of themselves. See it as a chance to learn something new about yourself, the other person, or the world around you. Where else in life do we get such a wonderful opportunity? Your dating experience will be what you make it. It can be fun and enjoyable or unpleasant and difficult. You have the choice. By way of a cautionary tale, we'd like to recount the story of Phoebe.

Phoebe – Runaway Expectations

After raising five children, Phoebe chose to divorce her husband of twenty-seven years. She hoped that she might find, in another relationship, all the passion and emotional fulfillment that her marriage had lacked. Phoebe had been considerably overweight for most of her life. After her divorce, she went to extreme measures to lose her excess weight and managed to lose most of it. It was quite an achievement, and she was feeling good about herself. She decided it was time for her to experience the exciting and passionate relationship she had always longed for. Her ideal man was an urban cowboy who was tall, handsome, muscular, wealthy, and most importantly, chivalrous. She imagined him to be the kind of man who wore cowboy boots and drove a luxury full-size pickup truck— her modern version of the strong, gallant knight on his valiant steed. When she came to us, she described this man, and we agreed that he sounded wonderful. However, we knew that both he and her projected feelings for him were fantasies. We told her that there was no harm in imagining a guy like this, just as long as she was aware that he was a fantasy. We reminded her that we were matchmakers in the real world, and in the real world, most actual cowboys lived at least a thousand miles from us and were not likely to meet the rest of her criteria. Yet, even if we couldn't give her this cowboy, we knew we could help her find all the love and passion she was longing for, with a wonderful man who actually existed. She smiled and nodded, and said that was what she really wanted.

Although Phoebe had lost a lot of weight, she still didn't have a great figure. But her transformation had both revealed her natural beauty and given her a zest for life. Phoebe was smart and expressive. She loved her kids, she loved live music, and she loved her job. We knew a number of terrific guys who would appreciate all she had to offer, and we were excited to introduce her to them. One of these men soon rose to the top of our list. Mark was just a few years older than Phoebe, and had a cool look about him. Though he was a little overweight, he was attractive with a great smile, baby blue eyes, and wavy salt and pepper hair. He was a smart, hard-working man who owned his own successful company. Both he and Phoebe were introspective and liked to talk about many subjects in depth. They shared so many interests, from traveling and exploring new places, to wine-tasting, to live music— especially country music. We knew they could have a lot of fun together, and we hoped there would be a great connection.

We planned a perfect evening for them. They would enjoy dinner on a beautiful tree covered patio, followed by live country music under the stars. We had set the stage for romance and, being sure they would have a wonderful time, we couldn't wait to hear how the evening would go.

It was a Saturday night and we were in the office working late when Phoebe's name appeared on the caller ID. It was only 7:20PM, and the date had been set for 7:00PM. We wondered why she would be calling. Had they missed each other? Was there a problem with the reservation we had made? Elizabeth answered the phone. On the other end of the line was the most unexpected experience that we have ever had in all of our years of matchmaking.

It was Phoebe all right, and she was sobbing so hard her words were impossible to distinguish. She sounded like someone who had just witnessed a horrible accident.

"Phoebe, oh my god, what's wrong? What are you saying?"

"It's . . . it's," (huge sob), "it's Mark!"

Elizabeth's face went white. "What happened? Was there an accident?"

"No, it's not that."

"Did he not show up?"

"He did, he's here."

"Then what's going on?"

After another bout of sobs, she managed to speak again. "He's here. He's here, oh, it's just so awful. He's huge! He's fat and he's old!"

Now we were concerned. We were worried that Mark was near enough to hear all of this. Phoebe explained that she was in the ladies' room. Hysterical, she kept repeating that Mark was fat and old and she knew that she was going to end up with someone just like that. Taking turns on the phone, we managed to calm her down. We explained that Mark was a wonderful man, that he wasn't as big as she said, and that he was, in fact, only a few years older than her. "Listen Phoebe, you need to pull yourself together and enjoy yourself," Elizabeth said. "You're there on the date. All right, maybe he's not right for you, but you're really going to hurt his feelings if you keep acting like this. Make it a nice date for him. You will probably enjoy the evening, if you give it a chance. We can talk later." Phoebe calmed down and said goodbye. Stunned, we looked at each other, mouths open, eyes wide.

The next day, Phoebe called again. She was still upset. She was still saying the same things. It dawned on us that, although she appeared confident, Phoebe had been putting up a front. The problem was not Mark's appearance. The problem stemmed from the fact that Phoebe had never really gotten over the issues that challenged the way she saw herself— her age, her figure, and her overall self worth.

When someone is looking for a person to help them feel better about themselves, they often wrap their self worth up in other people's appearance and status. They believe that finding an ideal partner will heal the part of them that they experience as unworthy. The reality is that this doesn't work. Another person's attributes can't bolster your self-esteem, and this kind of relationship is ultimately unsatisfying for one or both parties involved.

Feeling concerned, we called Mark. The poor guy had suffered through a terrible date. Phoebe had not been openly rude to him, but she was certainly standoffish and obviously disinterested. On top of this, she had downed quite a few glasses of very expensive wine. Mark felt he had wasted his time and money. Not, he explained, because he hadn't found a potential partner, but because the evening had been so unpleasant.

Phoebe's lack of emotional balance triggered an intense reaction as soon as she laid eyes on Mark. She had gone on the date with the kind of ridiculously high expectations that no real man could live up to. No wonder she came back down to earth with such a crash. Following the letdown, there was no way she could allow herself to enjoy the date. She had created the terrible disappointment of the evening for herself. According to Mark, the bands that played that night were some of the best he had ever heard. Due to her lack of emotional balance, Phoebe was deaf to them. It's not much of a stretch to guess that the fine wine she was drinking had also been soured by her mood. And as for the chance to meet a lovely, interesting, generous man— she blew it completely.

The evening had left Mark feeling frustrated and disillusioned with the dating process. Like many people, Phoebe was unaware that her actions and reaction had an impact on the other person involved. Mark, a generally level-headed guy, was knocked off balance by the experience. He later found love, but it took a while to repair the damage.

Phoebe went on several more dates with other men and did start a number of relationships. The first was with a successful, handsome man, who was younger than herself. However, her insecurity and lack of emotional balance drove him away within a few months. In another relationship, the man adored her, but she eventually dismissed him because he wasn't successful enough. Her sense of self-worth was so entangled in the external qualities of the men she dated that the relationships, like her date with Mark, were doomed from the start.

How can you avoid falling into the same trap that ruined Phoebe's date? Very easily. When you go on a date, don't let your expectations run away with you. Stay level-headed. When you look at the person across from you, make sure you understand that their success, looks, and lifestyle are their own and do not improve or downgrade yours. In the previous chapter, we explained that you generally need more than a few dates to get to know someone. In Phoebe's case, it must have taken her all of ten seconds to write off a great person. If the person you meet really doesn't correspond with what you are looking for, don't check out. Be gracious and treat them like you would want to be treated. Being a good date is always the best choice. Not only will you have a better experience, the person you meet will be left intact.

Finding and maintaining emotional balance will determine the quality of your experience in the dating world. When it comes down to it, a date is not that big of a deal. It's only an hour or two of your time, and that's all. Now measure that against your end goal. It's a drop in the ocean. Keep this in mind, and you will keep your perspective. Keep your perspective, and you will have a foundation for emotional balance. Master emotional balance, and you can make the best of *any* situation.

Dating with Perspective

The best way to approach dating is with the knowledge that there will be great dates, flat dates, and even bad dates. Of course, it is unpleasant when a date is disappointing. However, in the grand scheme of life, these disappointments are part of the process and will seem insignificant once you have found your life partner. If you go into any activity with unrealistically high expectations, you will inevitably encounter some kind of let down. To be ready to meet the love of your life, you need to be positive and enthusiastic when you go on dates. At the same time, you need to be realistic enough that a flat or unpleasant date does not upset you. Striking this balance is the *most* important, and indeed the *hardest,* request that we make of our clients.

You make better choices when you remain level-headed. As a result, balance impacts the quality of the relationships you end up in. Lack of balance can sabotage your dating efforts in many ways. One way is to let yourself become too excited about someone before you have spent sufficient time together and gotten to know enough about them. Too often, people become excited about someone based on just an email or two, a series of text messages, a few phone calls, or just one date. Even after several dates, it is important to remind yourself that you don't really know this person. You don't have enough actual experiences with them to determine that they are kind, responsible, or trustworthy. Are they someone who is able to build and maintain a relationship? Are they *actually* compatible with you? Determining these things takes time spent together *in person*. In the early stages of connecting with and dating someone new, we recommend adopting an "optimistic, wait and see" attitude. Engage in the dating process and enjoy it! Allow the relationship to unfold naturally. Take time to get to know this new person and give them time to demonstrate who they are. Only with time and shared experiences can you make a good choice about whether or not someone is the right life partner for you.

When we get caught up in our desire to find love, we often jump into relationships too quickly. We can make quick decisions that we later regret or come on too strong and scare someone away. Much too often, our clients meet someone they think is wonderful and immediately want to date them exclusively. We call this **Premature Loyalty**. Becoming exclusive too quickly has many risks. New relationships are fragile and the pressure of Premature Loyalty can weaken them and cause them to fail. Premature Loyalty is also like putting all of your eggs in one basket; it cuts out all other opportunities and isn't a productive way to reach your goal of finding a life partner. In time, you may realize that you have made the wrong choice. Meanwhile, all your other candidates will be gone, and you will have lost time, opportunities, and valuable emotional energy. Maintaining your balance and taking the time to get to know someone before you invest too much of yourself in a relationship will save you from the cycle of falling in love and breaking up over and over again. Dating exclusively is an important step when the time is right. However, your full romantic attention and time should be earned. Connections made in early dating are exciting, but real relationships take time to develop.

Logan – Simmer Down Ladies

A story about one of our favorite clients, a firefighter by the name of Logan, perfectly demonstrates the perils of Premature Loyalty and the necessity of emotional balance. Logan was handsome, funny, and outgoing. Coming to us after a broken engagement, he wanted the opportunity to meet many different types of women with the hope of finding one to settle down with. He was non-judgmental and very open. To Logan, each woman he met was a fascinating and wonderful person. The feedback we got from the women he met was always the same. He made them feel as though they were the only woman in the room. He swept them off their feet and left them smitten. As far as our progress with Logan was concerned, this was all great news. For the women, it was less so. Now remember, we get to hear both sides of every situation.

Logan was so charming that, in one day, three separate women came into our office to tell us they didn't want to meet anyone else. In each case, the women had only been on *one* date with him. One date, and these women were prepared to throw out all other potential partners and only date Logan. As wonderful as he was, each woman's choice to exclusively date him was way out of proportion to the reality of her situation. This kind of reaction is one example of Premature Loyalty. All aspects of their emotional balance went out the window. They fixated on Logan to the point where no one else mattered. *Logan didn't do anything wrong.* He didn't make any promises or advances. In fact, he was a perfect gentleman. He was just living in the moment and presenting his best self. But these women got so caught up in their own enthusiasm that they lost all perspective. Even if we'd been able to convince them to continue dating other men, there was no way anyone else would have stood a chance. By all means, get excited, be enthusiastic, enjoy the promise of potential happiness— but don't let your emotions get ahead of you and blind you to the reality of your situation.

You may meet someone and, after the first date, feel that they are special. You may even feel that they are "The One!" On the second, third, or fourth date, that same person may not be so amazing. Things you didn't notice the first time, like certain annoying habits or diverging values, might become apparent. Giving a positive experience too much weight can lead you in the wrong direction. It can burn out a relationship that had real potential. It can make us overlook warning signs or important incompatibilities and allow the wrong relationship to work *for a while.*

When all hope becomes attached to one person too soon, all fears become attached as well. As a result, even the smallest issues will often be blown out of proportion. If you decide that someone is "The One" before you really know them, and then they don't call exactly when they said they would, your excitement turns to unnecessary anxiety. Premature Loyalty will cause extreme ups and downs and will wear you out. It will use up your valuable time and emotional energy and make it difficult, if not impossible, for you to continue in your search.

Another reason for keeping emotional balance is to ensure that your last experience doesn't dictate the quality of your next. If you come home from a bad date (and there will be bad dates), don't dwell on it for too long, or it will infect your outlook and spoil your next date. Keep your emotional balance. Hold on to your perspective. Don't take offense too easily, or take things personally. Don't let an offhand remark or a simple misunderstanding become something irredeemably awful.

Without the Balance Predictor, it is easy to become upset when something trivial happens or doesn't happen. One woman we knew was mortally offended when her date didn't open the door for her at the restaurant. Fair enough, you may be disappointed by a lack of gallantry from a man you spend an evening with, but is it enough to write him off for good? During one of our classes, a woman was talking about a date she had been on earlier that week. She was upset because the guy hadn't looked as attractive in person as he had in his photo and their conversation was flat. She declared the date a "disaster." A disaster? Isn't that just a little bit of an exaggeration? "Really?! If they don't call FEMA, it's not a disaster!" Elizabeth told her. But seriously, if she considered *this* date a disaster, she would be in for a great deal of disappointment and a bumpy ride with all the ups and downs of dating. Also, can you imagine how the guy must have felt? No matter how good an actor you are, if you consider a few dull hours spent in someone else's company a "disaster," it's a fair bet that the person you are with will pick up on it. It is up to both parties to ensure that they are having a good time. Lack of balance will make you selfish and cut you off from other people. Be someone who leaves your date uplifted and emotionally intact. As we always say, "Leave them better for having met you." Be patient, be kind, be helpful to the person you are with. Remember that they are in the same situation as you are. If the simple courtesy of being nice to another human being is not enough, consider this: you never know who your date might know. A future client, employer, or even your life partner. Your reputation is on the line.

Emotional balance is a valuable asset, not just in dating, but in all areas of life. Found love? Great, now you have to keep it— emotional balance will help you. Going for a job interview?

Buying a house? Starting a new business? Emotional balance will guard you from the highs and lows of any endeavor. It will allow you to exercise clear and rational thought. It will help keep your energy levels steady and productive.

Finding Balance

Maintaining emotional balance is essential to reaching your dating goals— but easier said than done. When you are creating balance in your dating life, it's important to watch out for the following obstacles:

Stress – The speed of modern life can cause stress for even the strongest of us. Stress is the natural enemy of balance. It can zap your strength, twist your emotions, and knock you off-kilter. The most effective way to find emotional balance while dating is to manage stress, both throughout the dating process and in other areas of your life. When you are under stress, perspective can be lost. Minor issues become dramas, while serious concerns are often ignored. If you are experiencing stress in other areas of your life, it may be difficult to maintain a balanced perspective while dating and even harder to build a healthy relationship.

Negative Self-talk – Negative self-talk is another major obstacle to creating and maintaining emotional balance. What is self-talk? It is the dialogue we all carry on within our own heads as we assess the world, other people, situations, emotions, and events, past, present, and upcoming. Our self-talk exists to help us navigate the world and learn from past experiences. In this respect, it is like a protective parent whose wish is to keep us safe from real or imagined harm. Unfortunately, when left unchecked, this voice can often be overprotective and excessively critical. At times, our self-talk can even be incredibly cruel. For example, in examining a date, your self-talk might sound like: "How could I have said something so stupid?" "Why didn't I wear a different outfit? I look terrible in this!" "I should have kissed her. Now she is going to think I'm not interested. I'm an idiot!" Honestly, would you ever allow anyone else to talk to you in the same way you sometimes talk to yourself? Your inner dialogue can be less than uplifting and definitely distracting. If you are caught up in your own thoughts and concerns while you are on a date, you are really just on a date with yourself. When it comes to dating, negative self-talk diminishes your overall experience and your chances of connecting with someone.

Self-centricity – Another obstacle to maintaining emotional balance in your dating life is the pitfall of being self-centric. When you approach dating from a self-centric perspective, you are only concerned with your own experiences in the dating world. All too often, we see people approach dating in the same way as Phoebe did: as though they are the center of the dating universe. They only consider their own feelings, thoughts, and what they want out of situations. It's almost as if they don't even realize that the people they meet on dates existed before they walked into the room, will exist after they leave, and will be equally impacted by their interaction. This is being self-centric, and it is neither productive nor attractive.

Dating from a self-centric perspective will negatively impact your emotional balance by making every detail of every encounter feel like it means something about you and seem more significant than it is. For example: If you are on a date with someone who is distracted or doesn't seem friendly, you are likely to think something like "She's not interested in me," or "I only meet jerks." By being self-centric, not only will you end up making potentially incorrect assumptions about your date and the general dating pool, you will also likely ruin the date for yourself and for the other person.

A self-centric perspective can also misguide you on the opposite end of the spectrum. You may think that you and your date found each other attractive, shared a great evening, and feel excited to see each other again. Yet, in reality, you missed the cues that would have told you they were not having the same experience. Most often, dates viewed from this self-centric perspective will leave you at one emotional extreme or the other— either you will be upset, angry, and offended by a bad date, or smitten, excited, and swept off your feet by your fantasy. Over time, this self-centric approach, and the ups and downs it creates, can weaken your emotional balance and even erode your belief that you will find someone.

Fear of Judgment and Rejection – One of the most common concerns attached to dating is the fear of being judged and rejected. We have all experienced the fear that people will negatively judge our appearance, accomplishments, personality and social grace and then reject us as a result of those judgments. It is natural to want to be liked and even desired by someone we are interested in dating. But when this desire leads to a significant fear of rejection, it is an obstacle to emotional balance. When we fall into the trap of letting our fear take over, we have already lost our perspective and compromised our balance, and the effect on our dating goals is damaging.

Our fear of being judged and rejected can stop us from reaching out and meeting new people. Let's say you are at a coffee shop, and you see someone you have been wanting to talk to. Just as you are working up the nerve to say hello, your fear of their judgment and rejection overtakes you, and instead of going over to their table, you turn and walk in the other direction. Or maybe you are using an online dating site and come across a great profile. You reach out to the person, and they seem like someone you could really be interested in, so you begin exchanging messages. Just as you are ready to meet them in person, you start to fear that they might judge and reject you, and as a result, you stop responding to their emails. Losing your perspective and emotional balance and letting your fear take over can rob you of opportunities to find love.

When we are preoccupied with the worry of being judged and rejected, we are taken out of the moment and into our heads. We emotionally retreat from the situation, and it becomes difficult for other people to connect with us. Our dispositions and our demeanors change. We become nervous and self-conscious, our body language becomes tense and unwelcoming, and we are less comfortable to be around. Our fear causes us to put up walls and barriers that are hard to get past and keep us from expressing the best parts of ourselves— the parts that people can connect and fall in love with.

Managing the Obstacles and Maintaining Your Balance

You now understand how important emotional balance is to your success and are aware of its major obstacles. Our next step is to give you a guide that you can follow as you go through the dating process that will help you manage those obstacles and find your emotional balance.

Managing Your Overall Stress – The overall level of stress in your life has a direct impact on the stress you experience in the dating process. Creating ways to reduce your stress on a regular basis will have a huge effect on your ability to maintain emotional balance. There are many methods for alleviating life's day-to-day stresses. Some of the most popular and effective techniques include: meditation, exercise, walking, yoga, prayer, laughter, spending time in nature, being with uplifting friends, and helping others. Find a method that works for you— one that not only calms your mind and body, but also gives you pleasure and is something you enjoy doing. By keeping your stress level low in the other areas of your life, it will be easier for you to maintain your emotional balance throughout the dating process. Dating is an area of life in which we tend to be much more vulnerable and sensitive. When our stress level is low, we are better able to maintain perspective, handle the ups and downs, and avoid the obstacles that accompany the dating process.

Maintaining Balance Before a Date – One of the most effective ways to avoid stress before your dates is to create a pre-date routine. Plan ahead, and don't leave things to the last minute. Nothing is worse than realizing that the outfit you wanted to wear is in the laundry, that your car needs to be vacuumed, or that there is a major construction delay on the route to the restaurant right before a date. A few days ahead, make sure you have a plan for what you need to do to be ready for the date on time and in a great frame of mind. It is all about staying as relaxed as possible so that you can enjoy the date, be fully present, and let your best self show up.

The day of the date, set aside extra time to get ready. If you are meeting someone after work, try to go home, take a shower, and turn on your favorite music while you are getting dressed. This will help you put the worries of the work day aside and feel like a happy single person, ready for a fun evening out. If you can't stop at home before the date, bring a change of clothes to work— this will at least help you shift your energy and look your best. Relax, and get into a positive frame of mind.

Reducing your stress with a pre-date routine will help you to manage your fears. Before you leave for your date, let your fears wash over you; face them, reason with them, put them in their place. You are in charge, not your fears. If you have had disappointments in the past (as we all have), don't take them with you when you go on a date, and certainly don't project them onto your dating future. Stay focused on what is happening in the present and not on your concerns for the future. Avoid worries such as: Will she show up? Does he expect someone better looking? Will he call? Is this going to work out? and so on. These kinds of thoughts will achieve nothing except bring you down and throw you into emotional imbalance. Instead, reassure yourself with positive and uplifting thoughts: I'm going to have fun tonight. I'm excited to meet someone new. It's a beautiful night and I have always wanted to try this restaurant.

Maintaining Balance on a Date – It's important to remember that dating is not about judgments or rejections, but about finding someone to love and share your life with. No one goes on a date with the objective of judging or rejecting you— they are there with the hope that they can find love. How can someone judge or reject you when they don't know the real you? Of course you will meet people who don't want to date you, and keep in mind that you will meet people whom you don't want to have a relationship with, either. That's just fine. However, in neither case is the true person being judged or rejected.

Get out of your head and into the date! Be present with the person who is sitting across from you and avoid focusing on your internal dialogue. Set aside thoughts that distract you and undermine your confidence such as: Did I pick the right restaurant? Is she having fun? Is he into me? Is he noticing how bad my hair looks today? Just as importantly, don't preoccupy yourself with searching for signs that they could be "The One," or worrying about how compatible or incompatible you are. This is not the time to be analyzing details. You can do a full accounting of the evening when you get home.

Instead, focus on what is actually happening in the moment. Listen to what your date is saying with the intention of hearing them and understanding them. Whether or not you initially think that your date is your match, look for their good qualities: her sweet smile or his quiet confidence. Look for the best in people and you can find wonderful characteristics. Pay attention to the enjoyable moments and the good parts of the date: discovering a common passion for music, or even just the pleasure of a great meal.

When you shift your focus from yourself, you can keep your attention on making sure your date is having a good time. Being a good date feels good. By trying to ensure the comfort of the other person, you will experience feeling more balanced, more sure of yourself, and more calm. You will also be able to remember that a date is supposed to be fun. Recently one of our clients asked us, "What ever happened to just going out and having a good time?" Like Logan, live in the moment, put your best foot forward, and make sure you *and* your date enjoy the experience. If you're having a good time, it is much easier to make new connections and stress will no longer be an issue. Once you make this shift, you will find that emotional balance and perspective are much easier to retain and that each date is a much richer experience.

Maintaining Balance After a Date – When you come home from a date, it is important to keep yourself centered. Regardless of whether you had a great time and feel like you made a new connection, or you had a flat experience and aren't interested in seeing your date again, keep your perspective. If it wasn't a great experience, remember it was just one date— you will have future dates with people you connect with. On the other hand, if you had an amazing time and see potential for a great relationship, keep in mind that you really don't know much about this person yet, and you can't be sure if your feelings are lasting or even mutual. Don't jump ahead of yourself or the situation. Look forward to learning more about this new person, and stay open to whatever might develop between you on future dates. If after one or even a couple of dates, someone doesn't want to see you again, don't let the disappointment derail your dating progress. Don't take it personally. You simply weren't right for each other, and it doesn't mean anything negative about you or them.

Shifting your self talk can also make a difference in maintaining your emotional balance. Even when you aren't getting the results you want, you do have influence over how you feel about the dating process and your future. Create constructive self talk. Acknowledge the positive and good things you do. You went on a date that wasn't promising? So what? Say, "At least I got motivated. I got myself to meet someone new, and my next date will be better. I'm one date closer to finding my partner." or "He didn't call. That's OK— he must not be right for me." With this kind of self talk, you can move on more easily and, above all, you'll be able to stay in the dating process and reach your goal.

The dating process takes time. For some, the search may take months and for others, it may take years. Don't ever think you are wasting time meeting a new person. Every date you go on is a proactive accomplishment. If you want to think about wasting your time, consider all those hours spent mindlessly glued to the television. Being out in a nice environment with a new person and taking charge of your life is *not* a waste of time. You are one experience closer to finding your match.

We know how hard it can be to relax on a date— especially a first date! You may never completely dispel nervousness, or chase away all of your fears. This is normal and not a bad thing. But here is where perspective can make a huge difference. Some first dates are wonderful, some lots of fun, while others feel long and tedious. Whatever the experience or outcome, whatever you may feel or imagine the other person to be feeling, don't let your nerves take over. Try to keep in mind that a date is just a couple of hours spent giving yourself the opportunity to find love. And what's a few hours compared to the happiness of love?

So, whether it is preparing for a date or thinking over your last date, apply perspective. Find your inner balance. The Balance Predictor is the glue that holds the dating process together. Without The Balance Predictor, the other Predictors cannot be effective.

For dating and a healthy, happy life, **Balance is key.**

GETTING FROM SINGLE TO IN A RELATIONSHIP

THE VEHICLE PREDICTOR

GETTING FROM SINGLE TO IN A RELATIONSHIP
THE VEHICLE PREDICTOR

Our goals can only be reached through a vehicle of a plan, in which we must fervently believe, and upon which we must vigorously act. There is no other route to success.

–Pablo Picasso

WHAT DO we mean by vehicle? In everyday life, a vehicle is something that transports you from point A to point B. It is the mechanism you use to arrive at your desired destination. When we say Vehicle, we are referring to the various methods available for meeting other single people. Some examples of vehicles in the dating world include: online dating, speed dating, social connections, and matchmaking. We call them vehicles because they take you from being single to being in a relationship.

Why Do You Need a Vehicle?

People tend to think that love should just happen "naturally," and that taking planned steps to enhance their odds is unnatural, unnecessary, and desperate. Once, a potential male client said to us, "I feel like if I sign up with you, I will be falling on my sword." It is unfortunate that there has been a stigma attached to vehicles. Some people even believe that using them is a compromise or a failure. This could not be further from the truth. **No couple has ever met without a vehicle, whether they knew it or not.**

The Invisible Vehicle

Many of us begin our dating lives in our teens and early 20s, when meeting people is easy and new relationships begin all the time. Why is it so much easier to meet potential partners in our youth? Many people think it is just because we are young, usually at our most attractive, and baggage-free. But this explanation ignores some major realities about our environment at this stage of life. Unlike in other periods of our lives, as young adults, our peer group has a roughly 50:50 ratio of single men to single women. We are constantly surrounded by single people who are around our own age and with whom we share very similar experiences, including social scenes, classes, jobs, etc. We typically have more free time for a wider and more vibrant social life. Add the raging hormones of youth, and what do you get? The biggest and best *vehicle* for dating you will ever encounter in your life! Biology and society have combined to create the ideal vehicle for love to find *you*.

Think of the people you know who met their spouses and partners in young adulthood. They had an exceptional vehicle for finding love. Their vehicle was their environment. They just didn't know it.

When people find themselves unattached after their mid-twenties, they mistakenly expect their natural environment to continue to be rich with opportunities for love. We often find that people are stunned by how difficult it has become for them to meet potential partners. It is important to understand that, after young adulthood, critical aspects of our environment change and *that* is why it becomes so much more difficult to meet potential partners. After our mid twenties, more and more people are paired off leaving us with fewer available candidates. Our increasing job and personal responsibilities result in less free time to socialize. Then, as friends get married, have children, and lose interest in the singles scene, even our social opportunities dry up. With social circles that contain fewer and fewer singles and decreasing opportunities to meet potential partners, we lose our original vehicle. If you are serious about finding love, you need to replace that lost vehicle. If you are *really* serious about finding love, we recommend you replace it with a fleet of vehicles!

The stigma attached to using vehicles to find love comes from the simple lack of knowledge that you once had a vehicle, and you lost it. At about 16 years old, you were handed the keys to the Ferrari of dating vehicles. Then, somewhere in your late 20s, Father Time came along and repossessed that sweet ride. The plentiful opportunities of your early dating environment are no longer available. Therefore, it only makes sense to acquire new methods that create opportunities to find love. Now you know: you must replace your vehicle for connecting with other single people who are looking for love.

Choosing Your Vehicles

Love is looking for you, so you need to put yourself in places where you can be found. The more vehicles you have and the more adeptly you use them, the more opportunities love has to find you. In our experience, most people need multiple vehicles to reach their goal. The fewer opportunities you have to meet single men or women in your daily life, the more vehicles you will need. We generally suggest having *three vehicles*. If you have a rich social life where you regularly meet new single people, then two vehicles will usually do.

When choosing your vehicles, it is vital to consider whether they are right for you. The first major consideration is whether or not your vehicles suit your lifestyle. If you lead a busy life with long hours or frequent travel, choosing a vehicle that is time-intensive can be counter-productive. If your financial obligations do not leave you with much discretionary income, then it is best to look for low cost options. All vehicles require time and most require a financial commitment. Furthermore, they tend to have an inverse relationship, where the more time you spend on a vehicle, the less financial investment is necessary, and vice versa.

It is also important to make sure that the vehicles you choose compliment your personality and interests. This consideration is often overlooked, but crucial to your success. Your vehicles should highlight your best traits and work in favor of your strengths, rather than feel like chores or create additional challenges in your dating life. Here are a few examples. If you travel for work, then joining a co-ed softball league wouldn't be a good vehicle for you, since you would probably miss most of the practices and games. Instead, online dating or mobile apps would be great vehicles, since you can access them from anywhere, connect with people while you are away from home, and plan dates for when you return. On the other hand, if you are someone who doesn't like writing emails and you know that you won't respond to people in a timely manner, then online dating probably isn't the best choice. When people like your profile and contact you, you won't be able to make the most out of those opportunities. More productive vehicles for you would be social events, using a matchmaker, or joining a dating service, since they allow you to meet people without having to write and respond to emails. Likewise, if you are not very outgoing, then expecting to find success at large social events and parties could lead to disappointment. A better vehicle for you would be group events or classes, where the activities and introductions are set up for you. Choose the wrong vehicle, and you simply won't use it. You will squander your precious investments of time, money, hope, and emotional energy.

We also recommend choosing a variety of vehicles. Using different types of vehicles will give you access to a wider field of people and range of opportunities. For example, using a matchmaker, going to social events, and joining a co-ed community sports league, presents a naturally diverse mix. This combination will bring you more options than using three different kinds of co-ed sports leagues. Another good combination would be volunteering, online dating, and speed dating. The idea is to maximize your potential and to open your field as wide as possible with activities you enjoy. Using different vehicles not only helps your search for someone, it also puts you in the places where you can be found!

An important note about working with your vehicle: Working with your vehicle is like joining a gym. If you don't fully engage with the vehicle you choose, you won't get results. It doesn't work to simply sign up for an online dating site, but never check your account or return emails. No matter what kind or how many vehicles you use, it is never a passive action. When you use a car, you have to get in, make sure it has gas, turn the key, put it in gear and steer in the right direction!

Types of Vehicles

Below, we have compiled a diverse list of available vehicles. We have also provided information about each vehicle and how to get the best results using them. They are divided into five groups for ease of reference.

1. Networking, Connecting and Joining in:

One way to meet people is, of course, online. Social networking can reconnect you to old friends and open up new circles. Another way of networking is to join organizations and attend events in your community. Not sure where to start? Think about the things that are important to you. What kinds of organizations and activities reflect your values and interests? Are there specific interests that you want to share with your future partner? Using this first group of vehicles can be lots of fun in and of themselves. You can enjoy gratifying experiences and interesting activities while you are connecting with people. These methods will take a time investment, but because they generally involve things you are interested in, dedicated to, and care about, they should have the immediate benefit of enriching your life.

One advantage of joining organizations and clubs is that it is so much easier to find like-minded people who enjoy the same things you do. One challenge that these vehicles bring is that they are not exclusively for singles. You may choose to join a hiking club, only to realize that most of its members are married. Or you might arrive at an event, only to discover that not many people you are interested in chose to attend. Avoid getting involved with a group or club that doesn't offer many opportunities to meet people to date. It is important to make sure you keep moving forward and stay on task with your goal of finding love. Of course, if you enjoy the group, it's fine to maintain your membership. However, keep in mind: if the group isn't a vehicle for meeting your potential partner, you need to find an additional means of reaching your goal. If you try several groups or organizations, you should discover the ones that offer you good opportunities to meet other single people. Joining multiple organizations is fine, but don't spread yourself too thin. If you join too many groups, you may not have enough time to really connect with the other members. Networking is most successful when people begin to know, like, and trust you. Remember that it will take time and a sincere effort to connect within the group.

Below are some simple tips to remember so that you can get the most out of this type of vehicle:

— When you are deciding which group or club to join, make sure the members are the kind of people you would want to date.

— When picking a group or organization, think about the interests and activities that the people you want to meet might be drawn to. For example, if you are a woman, you may want to get involved with an organization that would attract men, like Habitat for Humanity. If you are a man, consider volunteering in the arts.

— Joining like-minded groups will bring you like-minded people. If you are political, think of choosing a group that represents your voice. If you are outdoorsy, look for a group that reflects your love of nature.

— Networking is about building relationships and adding to your network of contacts. You might not meet "The One" while networking, but you might meet someone who knows the perfect person for you.

— Always put your best foot forward. *Always.*

Options for networking, connecting, and joining in vehicles:

Networking: The people in your life already know and like you. They can be great advocates in your search for love. Invite them to help you find someone wonderful.

- Personal offline networking through family, friends, and acquaintances
- Business networking and professional groups and organizations
- Social networking

Connecting: We love this vehicle, because simply getting out in the world can make a huge difference. There are many options in this group. However, keep in mind that these are open venues and anyone can attend as they are not organized exclusively for singles.

- General social events, parties, sporting events, community festivals, etc.
- Bars, night clubs, dance clubs
- Seminars, personal growth workshops, adult education courses
- Groups and clubs for every kind of interest: these generally revolve around an affiliation, interest or hobby. Including but not limited to: country clubs, ski clubs, travel clubs, and other special interest clubs, Meetup.com groups, alumni groups, lodges, and the like.

Joining in:

- Faith Based Singles Groups: such organizations regularly hold meetings and events.
- Volunteerism: environmental groups, political groups, local nonprofits and charities. (Make a difference for someone else on your way to finding your partner!)
- Fitness activities, clubs, and facilities

An important note about the next four categories: The good news is that there has never before been so many ways to meet people! The bad news is that never before have they been needed so much. In our modern society, we have become increasingly isolated as individuals. Single people are left to fend for themselves in the search for love. This has lead to the creation of the Singles Industry. Innovative entrepreneurs have created new ways to connect singles, and these opportunities have continued to evolve and multiply. The advantages of utilizing these services and attending singles events are numerous. They are designed with singles in mind and they make it easier for people to connect. These services provide a platform for singles interested in dating, where it is much easier to move from small talk to a first date and romance.

2. Singles Events

Events designed exclusively for singles can be a great way to meet new people. They can be more effective than events for the general public or going out to bars and clubs. Everyone at these events is single (or they should be). Also, if they are hosted by professionals, the atmosphere and activities will be conducive to meeting new people and having fun.

When you are out in the world and attending singles events, try to utilize the following strategies:

— Be friendly, and remember to smile!

— Look your best.

— Be caught up on current events.

— Even if you are shy, make an effort to meet and talk to new people.

— Don't worry about saying the perfect thing— just make sure you interact with people.

— Put your phone away— its a signal to others that you don't want to be bothered and will keep people from approaching you.

—Keep in mind, it only takes one person to change your life!

Options for singles events vehicles:

- Professionally hosted singles events: speed dating, singles dinner parties, dances, singles cruises, and singles travel (The distinction for this category is that it's expressly intended for singles, and events are organized or hosted by professionals.)
- Personals and "Lonely Hearts" columns (This is less and less common in the United States, but still used in other areas.)

3. Online Dating and Mobile Dating Apps

Technology makes connecting with other singles convenient. When you use digital dating sites, you have access to your vehicle on your own schedule and from just about anywhere. The biggest advantage of online dating sites and mobile apps is the sheer number of people you have access to. Most of us know of more than one happy couple that met using an online service— it can work!

One thing to keep in mind when choosing to use these methods is their time-consuming nature. It can take a lot of effort to get offline and onto real world dates. If you choose these vehicles, it is important to be able to set aside plenty of time for your online search. Another factor to consider is that people aren't always honest in their online profiles or photos. When they aren't being honest, at best they are using old photos and embellishing their attributes in their profiles; at worst they are trying to scam kind-hearted people out of money or put them in physical danger. It is *very* important to protect your privacy, your identity, and your heart. Most dating sites have safety tips, and we strongly recommend that you follow them.

To get the most out of online dating and mobile dating apps, realize that your profile is a personal online marketing campaign. Any good marketing executive will tell you that you need to consider your audience. Think about what will catch their eye and capture their interest. Too often, people approach their profiles like they would a job application where they simply list their history and experience. Others forget their audience and include details that would more likely attract a new buddy and not a romantic partner. Generally, women write profiles that would appeal to other women, and it's the same for men. For example, people often list their hobbies. For women, it might be interior decorating, sewing, shopping, etc., but these activities, while they may be interesting to you, are not typically of great interest to men. Similarly, men proudly display their interests: endlessly watching sports, cars, fishing, hunting, drinking, etc. Great if you want to make a new best friend, but not something that generally attracts someone for a romantic relationship. The trick is to appeal to the people you want to meet. If you are a woman who enjoys (or doesn't mind) watching sports, make sure you say that. And guys, if you take pride in your home or value emotional maturity, for goodness sake, let the women know!

This is how you attract your target audience. We're not saying you should lie or list interests that don't appeal to you— just be mindful of activities that the opposite sex will want to share.

Here are some valuable suggestions for digital dating:

— Have great photos, have great photos, have great photos! Yes, we said that three times. Selfies send the wrong message. Have a friend take a good photo of you. It can also be worthwhile to use a professional photographer, as your photos are the most important part of your profile.

— Write a profile that will appeal to the people you are interested in meeting.

— Make time to do the work that is involved in using an online dating site or mobile app: browsing the members, sending and responding to emails, and setting up times to talk on the phone or meet in person when the time is right.

— *Always* be careful, *protect* your identity, and be *safe*. Never give out any details about where you live or work, or any information you feel uncomfortable sharing.

— Don't get into long emailing or texting relationships. You want a partner, not a pen pal.

— Make sure you don't fall in love with a fantasy. Understand that you can't actually *know* someone based on who they are online or even over the phone. **You need to spend time with them in person.**

— There is no such thing as an online date...dates happen out in the real world. (Of course, those dates need to happen in a safe, public place.) **You can** *search* **for love online, but you need to** *fall* **in love in person.**

Options for online dating and mobile dating apps vehicles:

- The Major Sites: These are the big online dating sites that have a general membership and very large numbers in their databases. These sites tend to have excellent software that makes using them easy and effective.

- Niche Sites: These are sites that specialize in a specific population. These populations include: religious, geographical, political, interest or lifestyle based, etc. They generally have much smaller membership numbers than the major sites, but offer more specific potential matches.

- Free Sites and Apps: There are some sites that don't charge a fee for their basic membership, and some are completely free of charge. Most sites will allow you to create a free profile, however, they may limit communication to subscribing members.

- Personality Test Sites and Apps: Some sites require that you fill out a personality questionnaire before creating a profile. Others allow you to add personality analysis to your profile. Each site handles this differently.

4. Offline Dating Services

The modern brick and mortar dating services began in the 1980s with video dating. Customers had video profiles recorded on VHS tapes, which would then be viewed by other singles. Today there are many varieties of offline dating services and they offer numerous ways for people to meet in person.

One advantage of using a dating service is that it isn't as time consuming as some of the other vehicles. Some services select who you will meet and set up the dates for you, while others let you do this yourself. Some of them promise a specific number of dates, while others allow you to contact people in their database with no guaranteed number of introductions. This can mean you get lots of dates, few dates, or even no dates at all.

To get the most out of working with a dating service, there are a number of things to keep in mind:

— Each service is a little different. It is important to ask about their individual policies and procedures and make sure that what they offer is a good fit for you.

— Be open and clear about the kind of people you want to meet.

— Approach each date with an optimistic attitude.

— Be sure to give detailed and reflective feedback after your dates.

5. Personalized Matchmaking Services

Matchmaking has been part of society for a *very* long time. Many cultures employ the time-honored tradition of using a respected member of the community to help find suitable spouses for single men and women. Today's matchmakers have the same goals, but in this modern world, singles have modern wants and needs, and matchmakers use modern methods.

If you choose to work with a matchmaker, know that you have chosen a powerful vehicle. We feel that matchmaking is an exceptional vehicle, and our reason for saying this is not simply because it is our chosen career. The vast majority of skilled matchmakers are dedicated professionals who provide expertise and experience no other vehicle can offer. If you use this vehicle, choose a matchmaker you feel comfortable with, and who you believe has your best interests at heart. The rapport between you and your matchmaker is an essential part of the process. Your relationship should be one of trust, patience, and cooperation.

Among the many advantages of matchmaking is the distinction that a matchmaker looks for your husband, wife, or life partner— not just a date. This is extremely important because matchmaking is the only sector of the singles industry that works *exclusively* with people who want to find "The One."

Other services accept members who are also interested in casual dating. This difference is part of what makes matchmakers so successful, as all of the people they work with have the same goal. Matchmakers also work closely with their clients to understand who their clients are as individuals and what kinds of people they want to meet. Then, like an executive recruiter, matchmakers conduct searches for the best candidates and arrange the introductions.

To fully capitalize on working with a matchmaker, follow these guidelines:

— Make sure you are entirely open and honest with your matchmaker.

— Be amenable to constructive feedback, be it positive or negative, and to coaching.

— Be ready and willing to meet all of the people your matchmaker suggests for you.

— Make going out with your matches a priority.

— Be positive and optimistic about every introduction, and trust that your matchmaker chose this person for a good reason.

— Bring the best version of yourself to each introduction.

— Be patient as your matchmaker searches for your match; a great deal of effort goes into finding and arranging dates.

— Maintain your emotional balance throughout the process!

Date Coaching – Enhancing Your Vehicle's Performance

Successful athletes use coaches to help them to improve their performance. Executives work with business coaches to reach higher levels of excellence. Dating coaches give singles these same kinds of advantages in the dating world. If you choose to work with a dating coach, you will be receiving one-on-one training in how to successfully date and get the best possible results. A dating coach functions as a guide, helping you to first identify and move beyond the barriers that have kept you from reaching your relationship goals. With the guidance of a professional coach, you can break any obstacle or pattern you are encountering, such as:

— Going on lots of first dates, but not many second ones
— Always dating the "wrong kind" of people
— Staying too long in unfulfilling relationships
— Dating a lot, but not getting into serious relationships
— Getting into lots of short term relationships, but not reaching the goal of marriage.

A dating coach can also help you use your vehicles more effectively. Whether you decide to use online dating, join a social group, or work with a matchmaker, dating coaches can give you a wide range of information and help you develop skills that can improve your experience and your results. No matter what vehicles you choose, dating coaches are uniquely equipped to support you and help you get the most out of using them. Some of the topics an experienced dating coach can help you with include:

• Dating safety
• Best dating practices
• How to create digital dating profiles that are effective in reaching your goals
• Image consulting
• Connecting and communicating with the opposite sex
• Increasing your confidence

In addition, a dating coach can be a great resource for helping you apply the Six Predictors to your search. A coach can keep you accountable to your *priority* of dating, support you in strengthening your *belief,* encourage you to stay *open* to new opportunities, help you stay centered and maintain *balance,* assist you with evaluating your *vehicles*, and help motivate you to stay in **action**.

The dating world can be difficult and confusing. Having an expert advisor can help your vehicle run more smoothly, improve the experience of your journey, and help you arrive at your destination more quickly.

The Pitfalls of Modern Dating

As we have said, there has never been a better time to be single. There are more vehicles now than ever before to help you meet potential partners. However, new dating vehicles inevitably bring with them new hazards. Thanks to the leaps and bounds of technology, not only do we have more *ways* to meet people, but the *amount* of people we are able to meet has multiplied many times over. As a result, there are new challenges to overcome and new bad habits to steer clear of. With each new means of meeting people, new problems can arise. Make sure to avoid falling into these traps:

The Kid in a Candy Store – With digital dating, you can have millions of candidates right in front of you. The trap is that you can start out excited by all the choices, but then find yourself caught up in the excitement and, inevitably, confused. It's better to focus on a manageable number of people who might be all-around good matches for you, rather than lots of people just because you can. If you are trying to communicate with too many people, you won't have the focus or energy to invest in actually connecting with the people who have real potential. We have seen many clients delight in how many different people send them emails and text messages, and then fail to cultivate the online flirtations into real world relationships.

The "Next" Mentality – This trap is a symptom of our modern age of disposability, which causes us to cast aside perfectly appropriate suitors simply because there *might* be a more desirable option. We are always envious of the newest model and the latest gadget. As a result, we dispose of what we already have in the hope of finding something better. Always remember what you are looking for, make sure you can recognize it when it's in front of you, and, by all means, don't throw it away. We once had a client who carelessly passed on relationships with a number of good men. She later told us that she thought of dating like she thought of real estate: What's next to see? That may work in real estate, but it certainly doesn't work in dating!

Taking Dates for Granted – The mere fact that we can meet so many new people means that we easily fall into the trap of devaluing dates— both the experience and the individual. Just because you have five first dates lined up this month, don't treat any of them as less important than the others. Each new person has the potential to be the love of your life, and it just might be that the first one is the right one. Make sure you are paying attention and giving yourself a chance to truly connect on each and every date.

Now that you know the ins and outs of choosing your vehicles, working with them, and avoiding their traps, we would like to tell you the inspiring story of a former client, Lily. She used her vehicles to completely change her dating life. With our guidance, she chose three vehicles that suited her personality and lifestyle, committed her time and energy to working with them, and avoided the pitfalls of modern dating.

Lily – In High Gear

When she came to us, Lily was in her mid 30s. A doctor working in a very specialized field, Lily was highly educated, had dedicated her life to her work, and enjoyed a position of great prestige. Yet, despite all of her accomplishments, she was unhappy. Lily felt that she couldn't enjoy her successes because she hadn't found fulfillment in the one area of life she considered the most important. She told us that, when she thought about her life, she was shocked that she had gotten this far without love. She had never married and her past relationships had all been difficult and had ended in disappointment. Each of the men she began relationships with had promised her love and honesty, and each and every one of them had let her down. Sitting in front of us, telling us her history, we could feel her heartache as she told stories of betrayal and rejection. She said to us, "I'm so afraid that love will always be something that just hurts me, and I'll never meet a man who I can trust." As she talked, her eyes welled up with tears, but, saying she was "all cried out," she wiped them away. Lily had decided to stop feeling sorry for herself and become proactive. She had decided to make a change in her life. She wanted marriage and kids. She was ready to make it happen. But the problem was she didn't know *how*.

Lily hadn't dated anyone seriously in five years. She explained that her recent attempts to find love hadn't progressed beyond signing up for an online service and a few half-hearted comments to friends about wanting to meet someone. We explained the principle of needing vehicles, the wisdom of taking on more than one, and the importance of giving them her time and energy. We told her that we would gladly accept her as a matchmaking client. We assured her that signing up with an online dating service was a good choice, and we promised to coach her on how to get the most out of that vehicle. Seeing that she was a social person, we also recommended that she take part in our exclusive social club for single women, The Ms. Club. This club would provide regular singles outings and would be a wonderful and unique vehicle for meeting great men in a positive environment. Moreover, we knew this club would have an uplifting effect on her by supporting all of her dating efforts and building her confidence through education and friendship. By the end of the interview, we were able to point out that she now had three vehicles: our matchmaking, the Ms. Club, and the online dating service. "I do, don't I?" she said, smiling. We noticed her posture straightening and her confidence already returning.

As a matchmaking client, Lily was a joy to work with. We matched her with several men who shared her values, had similar life goals, and whom we knew she would enjoy meeting. Meanwhile, Elizabeth got to work on revamping Lily's online profile. Coming from a marketing background, Elizabeth has a unique understanding and expertise for this vehicle. As she says, "Online dating is a misnomer. There are is no such thing as online dating. Dates don't happen online— it's all just marketing yourself." Elizabeth explained to Lily that what she had to remember when writing her profile was who she was writing it for. She reminded Lily that men were her target audience and that what she wrote about herself needed to capture their attention. Lily had highlighted her interest in the arts and book clubs, but failed to mention that she loved hiking, whitewater rafting and college sports. We added those interests and deleted the book clubs— which would be of interest to other women, but were unlikely to create a connection with most men.

And then there were her photographs. Elizabeth explained to Lily that, in this area, less is definitely more. Lily had posted about seventeen images of herself, and not all of them were particularly flattering. Some of the photos were taken from below eye level, which lead to some double chins and up-nostril views, and some had bad lighting that made her look shiny and washed out. Others depicted Lily with several friends, which, Elizabeth pointed out, was distracting and potentially confusing for the men viewing her profile. We set up a photo session with our photographer, who made sure she highlighted Lily's femininity and most flattering features. Using a few of the professional photos and a couple of Lily's best snapshots, Elizabeth helped whittle the pictures down to 5 great images. The result of this profile makeover was immediate. Suddenly, Lily started getting a lot more attention on the site. Better yet, it was from the kind of men she was interested in meeting. Since we had written about her interests in outdoor activities like hiking and whitewater rafting, she was contacted by strong, confident, and active men, who were looking for a woman like Lily who shared their interests. Likewise, since she put more care into the image she projected in her new photos, more of the men who reached out to her were were guys who put thought into their appearance.

As for her third vehicle, Lily embraced The Ms. Club wholeheartedly. She became close with the other members who were having similar experiences with dating. These new friends made her feel like she wasn't alone and was surrounded by people who could relate to her. Together, they participated in our monthly classes. Lily learned about flirting, how to read body language, how to be confident in social situations, and how to use the The Six Predictors. She improved her dating skills and became empowered in her search for love. She became playful and fun around new people instead of falling back on her default serious and reserved nature. She got real-world practice when she attended the Ms. Club's monthly mixers. These cocktail parties and happy hours were held at comfortable and relaxed venues like intimate wine bars, upscale breweries, and trendy bistros where people could mingle and make new connections. As Lily began using her new skills, she enjoyed meeting men in these fun, low-pressure environments.

All the while, we were sending Lily out on introductions. In the beginning, the guys were telling us that she was quiet and seemed uptight and negative. They said that they didn't want a second date because, even though she was "cute," or "had an attractive personality," they didn't have fun or feel a romantic connection with her. But as time went by, we were excited to see that the feedback we received from the men Lily met was getting better and better with each date. As her dating experiences and results rapidly improved, men were asking her on second dates and telling us that they found her to be easy to talk to, smart, and fun to be with.

A few months after Lily had first sat in our office, we were finishing up one of our Ms. Club classes when Lily pulled us aside to tell us that she was truly happy. It was the first time she had actually *enjoyed* dating since high school, and even her friends and family could tell that she was happier. Her outlook on dating had changed. She was hopeful. She had a spring in her step and her laughter was infectious.

The next time we met with her, she told us, "It's just amazing! Over the last three weeks, between all of your matchmaking, my online dating, and the Ms. Club events, I have gone on fifteen dates and I've enjoyed all of them! Before each date, I remind myself that this could be the night I meet my future husband. I also tell myself to relax, enjoy the evening, and know that if he isn't the one I am looking for, that's OK."

She continued all of her dating efforts for a few more weeks and found three men she felt had potential. One of them, Jake, had asked her to date him exclusively. Before she chose to set the others aside, she wanted us to help her decide if dating him exclusively was the right choice. We talked a little, but it was clear that she was already reaching her own decision. Jake had already begun to steal her heart, and now she was ready to fully give it to him.

When Lily came to us, she had seemed completely disheartened and unconvinced that she would find a life partner. Within four months, she had turned her love life around. Yes, it was quick, but we helped her choose vehicles that would work for her, and she truly committed to them in a powerful and positive way. Before we knew it, she and Jake were engaged. She told us that all of the effort, facing her fears of being betrayed and rejected, learning the Predictors, and going on date after date, was completely worth it!

Sticking with Your Vehicles

Lily's story is empowering and makes a great case for committing to your vehicles so that you can make the most of them. However, it's important to note that her journey is unique in how quickly she reached her goal. Some of the most serious and common obstacles people encounter when they work with their vehicles are their unrealistic expectations. Many people believe that simply having a vehicle will bring them quick success, and then become frustrated when reaching their goal takes longer and more effort than they expected. It is important to remember that most of the time, even with the best vehicles, results take time and persistence. As we've said, the search for love is a journey, not an event. Love usually does not happen immediately, nor without effort, just as in the real world we have not devised a mode of transport that can instantaneously move us from point A to point B. Far too often we see people expect immediate results from their vehicle, even though they are unwilling to commit their time and energy to the process. This is a symptom of our modern society's expectation that everything we want should be available here and now and with little effort. Love is not a commodity that can be ordered on Amazon and delivered the very next day.

You will need to engage with your vehicle regularly. Just like a car can't drive itself, your dating vehicle can't find love for you without your participation. There is no point hiring a matchmaker if you are going to ignore their advice and not put your best foot forward on dates. Likewise, why join a special interest club if you aren't going to attend the events and meetings? Why sign up for an online dating site and waste time plowing through profiles if you don't make an effort to communicate with the people you find interesting? Whatever vehicle you are using, it is never a passive experience. When people don't find a relationship as quickly as they had hoped, they have a tendency to blame the vehicle. It is fine to question if the vehicle you have chosen is right for you; however, to throw up your hands and yell, "This doesn't work!" is simply unproductive. Know that with *any* vehicle, your results will match your level of commitment.

Sometimes, when people become frustrated with online dating, they blame the site and the other members. They will complain that it takes too much time, doesn't have enough people, attracts the "wrong kind" of members, etc. Matchmakers too, experience clients' frustration when they don't get the quick fix they're looking for. One man who worked with us conveyed his frustration when he hadn't found love as quickly as he expected. He questioned us: "Why isn't this working? I never had these problems when I was younger. I'm quite a catch! Why isn't it *working*?"

Sometimes it just takes time— for that client, it took longer than he wanted it to. This upset him. He wanted to blame us, but deep down, he knew we were doing our job, and he stuck with it. Close to twenty months from when he began working with us, he got engaged to a woman who was the love of his life. For him, it took almost two years. For his fiancée, it only took two dates. Imagine that— only two dates to find love!

No one can ever predict how long finding love will take, so don't put yourself under the pressure of a deadline. No one can foresee who will find love on their second date and no one can anticipate who will take two years to meet the right person. What we do know is that if you have vehicles that can get you to your destination, and you commit to them, give them enough time to work, and don't give up, you are much more likely to find love.

Staying Roadworthy

Take time when choosing your vehicles. Research the vehicles available to you and select those that are most appropriate for your personality, your availability, and your finances. To get the most from your vehicles, realize that you are investing in yourself, your happiness, and your future. Treat them like an investment, and budget time and money for the vehicles you choose. Vehicles not only help you search for someone, they also put you in places where *you* can be found. That's a compelling point. You are not the only one doing the searching— your match is somewhere out there looking for you, too! Help them find you! How likely is it that you will meet your future love if all you do is sit on your sofa? Unless the love of your life is the UPS delivery person, he or she isn't going to come knocking on your door. *Get out there.* See and be seen. And what better way to get around town than in your customized, optimally running vehicle?

Like any journey, your search is not just about the destination. Keep in mind that each vehicle is an opportunity for personal growth and expanding your horizons. Not only will your vehicles help you find the love you seek, they can also be a way of enriching your life and preparing you to be in that relationship. We want you to find the happiness you long for, and we also want you to enjoy the process. Nothing is a waste of time if you enjoy doing it and you do it with conviction.

Above all, be encouraged! It is a wonderful time to be dating as there are more ways to meet people than ever before. Find the vehicles that best suit you, and get on the road to happiness!

So Much More than Just
Doing It
The Action Predictor

So Much More than Just Doing It

The Action Predictor

"Just do it!"

–Nike

(It's good advice, but there is more to the Action Predictor than just doing it.)

ACTION IS the necessary step that moves you from thinking about doing something to *actually* doing it. Of course, it may seem obvious that you will need to take actions to move your dating life forward. You know you will have to do things like meet new people, go on dates, and follow up with them. Yet time and time again, we see people start the dating process with enthusiasm and energy, only to let it stall out. We have to ask: Why does this happen? Why do so many people start with the best intentions, but somehow come to a standstill and fail to reach their goals? Consider that what might be missing is The Action Predictor. If your efforts seem disproportionate to your results, and you feel like you are engaged in the dating process but you aren't getting closer to your goal, ask yourself this: Am I bringing action to each of the Predictors? Are my actions supporting or hindering the other Predictors?

What we know is this: when someone has all of the other Predictors in place, but still struggles to find love, they are usually missing The Action Predictor. (When we refer to someone having a Predictor in place, we mean that they are effectively utilizing that Predictor in their search for love.) If Balance is the glue that holds The Six Predictors together, then Action is the energy source that moves them all forward. All of the other Predictors need to be plugged into Action to make them fully operational. Action is what takes you from just *thinking* about The Predictors to actually *implementing* them in your dating process. Likewise, Action depends on all of the other Predictors. Only when the other Predictors are in place can your actions be effective. Without the other Predictors, your actions will be wasted, and they can even take you in the wrong direction.

This is the essential point: All of the other Predictors depend on Action, and Action depends on all of the other Predictors. For example: You have to take the action of choosing to make your search for love your priority. Once you have made your search for love your priority, you will enthusiastically adjust your schedule and set aside time for meeting new people and going on dates.

We have created a written model to help you better understand this symbiotic relationship. Use this model when you are determining how to bring Action to each of the other Predictors and to help you understand how the Action Predictor will make the difference in your search for love.

Priority: I take the action of choosing to make my search for love my priority. Once I make my search my priority, my priority will influence and support my actions.

Belief: I take the action to understand my negative beliefs and the action to create and cultivate positive beliefs. Once I create positive beliefs, my positive beliefs will influence and support my actions.

Open: I take the action to consider where I am closed off to love and the action to become open to both the kind of person I can fall in love with and how love might occur in my life. Once I have become open to love, my openness will influence and support my actions.

Balance: I take the action to evaluate where I am not emotionally balanced and take the actions to create perspective and maintain emotional balance in my dating experience. Once I have developed emotional balance, my balance will influence and support my actions.

Vehicle: I take the action to research and choose the best vehicles for me. Once I have my vehicles, my vehicles will influence and support my actions.

It is amazing how Action and the other Predictors depend on and influence each other. Throughout this chapter, we will continue to examine their relationship and how you can use the Action Predictor to reach your dating goals.

Hilary and Thomas – The Late Date

Still not sure how the other five Predictors impact your ability to take actions and influence the quality of your actions? Then let us to tell you a story about a couple who just might have a chance to fall in love if, and only if, their actions don't mess it up. *Watch for how their Belief and Balance influence their Action Predictors and their dating experience.*

Hilary has a dinner date with Thomas and he is late. That's all that has happened. While she is waiting for him at the restaurant, she has lots of thoughts:

"He doesn't respect me, or my time."

"He doesn't really want to go out with me."

"He is a workaholic and has no work/life balance."

While she is waiting, she decides to work on some emails. When he finally arrives, he rushes into the restaurant, excited to see Hilary. (Thomas is about to experience Hilary through her actions, which are shaped by her thoughts and emotions.) He sees her checking her email on her phone. Since she feels he didn't respect her time, she decides to finish what she is doing. She says, without making eye contact, "I'll be just a minute. I need to finish this email." That makes him feel unimportant and he begins to think thoughts like:

"Hilary isn't that interested in me."

"She is probably emailing another guy."

"She's a workaholic. She doesn't have work/life balance and won't have time for me."

Feeling his interest waning and not wanting to waste time, he then says to her, "Why don't we just sit at the bar and have a drink."

Let's take a look at this scenario. What actually happened? He was late, and she was passing the time on her phone. That's it. However, they both let their negative beliefs and lack of emotional balance influence their next actions, turning what could have been a great date and a budding relationship into the reality of their fears. If we follow their thought processes further, they might sound something like this:

"Dating is a waste of time."

"This always happens to me."

"All the good ones are taken."

"If he's not serious about meeting someone, why did he even go on a date with me?"

"I need a break."

Without the Belief and Balance Predictors, thoughts like these can easily occur and usually lead to Action stalling out. The desire to find love then turns back into just a hope and a wish. The danger of disempowering belief and losing your emotional balance is that it creates negative thinking that can cause you to walk away from your goals. Be deliberate and conscious of your thoughts; they influence your actions and create your future.

How could the story of Hilary and Thomas have gone differently? Let's join them again at the start of their evening. Hilary is waiting at the restaurant for Thomas to arrive. He's late and she is wondering why. She thinks to herself:

"Maybe he worked a little late to finish something up. I know he is dedicated and has strong work ethic."

"He might be stuck in the construction traffic. Maybe it's something else. I am sure it will make for good conversation when he gets here."

She decides to relax and catch up on some emails while she waits. When Thomas arrives she looks up, smiles, and says, "Hi, it's great to see you! Let me just finish this and hit send." Thomas notices that her smile is more beautiful than he remembered, and thinks to himself that sitting in that horrible traffic jam in the construction zone was worth it to see Hilary again. He then goes up to the maître de and asks for a beautiful table by the window.

Like Hilary and Thomas, we all experience our actions being affected by the other Predictors. It's remarkable how positive belief and emotional balance can influence our actions, and how the results of those constructive actions can make the difference on a date and in a lifetime.

Thinking Versus Doing

While thinking about your goal and planning how to achieve it are fine, there comes a time— sooner rather than later— when you have to stop thinking and start *doing*. This is the Action Predictor. This is putting all the Predictors into practice at once. If you allow yourself too much time simply dreaming about your ideal partner, you're going to find yourself continually waking up in an empty bed.

We often encounter people who believe that they are actively engaged in looking for love, yet most of their activity is cerebral. They confuse the time and energy spent thinking about dating with the reality of taking actions in the real world, where their efforts can make an impact. Finding love doesn't happen between your ears. It happens between two people out in the world. Out there, beyond your head, is where love and the person you seek exists. Even if you are applying all five of the other Predictors, without The Action Predictor, your search for love won't get very far.

Melissa – The Illusion of Doing

Let's look at how Melissa was taken off course in her search for love by confusing thinking with doing. *Watch for how Melissa's lack of Action affected her Belief, her Balance, and her Vehicle Predictors.*

We liked Melissa the moment we met her. She had just turned 60 when she came to us for help in finding love. She was sweet, energetic, and worked in a caring profession. She referred to herself as "something of an old hippy, only without the drugs." She regularly meditated and approached life with a positive attitude. Divorced a number of years, she had decided it was time to return to the world of dating and the search for love. Her daughter had met her husband using a dating site, and she was pushing Melissa to give it a try. Less tech savvy than her daughter, Melissa decided to take one of our classes about online dating to see if it was right for her. She enjoyed the class, but still didn't feel confident enough to go it alone and asked if we would consider coaching her privately.

The next week, she met with us at our office and we got to know her better. By coming to us, we could see that she was making the search for love her priority and was allowing it to take precedence in her life. She admitted that a friend had finally lost patience with her selfless nature and ordered her, in no uncertain terms, to put herself first for once. In her work as a therapist, she promoted love every day of her life, and she held a firm conviction that she deserved to have a love of her own. Her Belief Predictor was unquestionable. When we asked her what kind of man she was looking for, she gave a big shrug and said,

"I know he's out there, I know I'll find him, but I'm not going to try to decide who he is before I have met him." So, being open was not an issue. Her experience dealing with distressed people in difficult situations in her work had given her a strong sense of perspective. With her practice of meditation and easy-going nature, it was clear that she had emotional balance. Taking our class was a good sign she knew she needed a vehicle. As for taking action, the fact that she had come to us with all the other Predictors in place made us confident that she was the kind of person who would follow through with her commitment and engage with the task at hand... or so we thought.

The next step was to help her choose the online dating site that was best for her and put together a great online profile. We helped her write about herself and her interests. We sent her to a professional photographer, who took photos that highlighted her fun, feminine, carefree nature. We reminded Melissa to follow our safety tips and guard her identity. Having given her all the tools she needed to succeed, we sent her off with high hopes. Melissa was ready for an adventure, and we were excited to hear about her results.

We checked in with her from time to time. A few months and a number of dates down the line, we got in touch by phone. She sounded a little flat and not at all like the woman we had met. She was apathetic and vague about her chances of meeting a great guy and didn't seem to want to talk about dating. We told her she needed to come see us. Begrudgingly, she agreed.

A few days later, Melissa was sitting in our office. She was smiling and laughing and had greeted us with her usual big hugs. We chatted pleasantly for a while about this and that, but when we turned to the subject to dating, her expression and mood changed. She told us that, yes, she had been meeting some nice men. Yes, she was pleased with how we set her up on the dating website. All the same, we could tell that, when it came to dating, a great change had taken place within her.

When this kind of thing happens, we become concerned. We asked Melissa if she'd had a bad experience with someone.

"No, not at all! Most dates have been nice and the others have at least been OK."

We asked her if she had received some bad news lately or if something was worrying her.

"Oh, no nothing really."

Then what was it? What had turned her enthusiasm to apathy?

She sighed. Her shoulders slumped. Looking at the floor, she started to tell us.

"I'm tired. I'm just . . . I'm tired."

This was very unlike Melissa, at least the Melissa we had first met. We pressed her to tell us more.

"It's exhausting. Dating is so much hard work. You know? I . . . I feel like I need a break. It's not just the dates. The dates are fine, I have fun, I laugh. It's not that, although they are getting harder to get excited about."

Well, if it wasn't the dates, what was it?

"All of it!" she exclaimed at last, looking up at us with an expression of frustration. "Just all of it. It's so tiring, all the time, every day, so much to do. I don't know if I can keep going like this. I know it's hard work. I know I can't expect to just walk into a loving relationship, but I didn't think it would be like this."

Gently, we encouraged her to explain what she meant. For Melissa, the experience of looking for love felt like a full time job that demanded her utmost attention and was draining her energy. But what, we insisted, was so tiring?

"Well, there's going on the dates... and..." she frowned at us, as if we should have known what she was trying to say.

"And what, Melissa?"

"And... I don't know. All the other things."

"Such as?"

Her eyes glazed over and she stared at us with a blank expression. "You know what? I don't even know what it is that's making me so tired."

We asked her how much time she was putting into online dating. She admitted that she only checked her online account once a week and hadn't replied to any emails in the past two weeks. From what she was telling us, other than going on a date here and there, we could see little evidence of this exhausting effort she felt she was putting in. We continued to ask her questions about all the dating related activities she could possibly be engaged in. She shook her head "No" to all of them.

The longer we talked, the truth of the matter became clear to Melissa: she wasn't actually doing much of anything to find love. She had been so wrapped up in the idea of finding love that her mind was in a constant state of flux with thinking about ways to achieve her goal. When her attention and mental focus wasn't required for work or other important activities, she thought about how to make love a reality. Not just thinking about it the way one might idly consider what to have for dinner while sitting in afternoon traffic— Melissa was dedicating most of her mental energy to code-cracking this dating problem. She had been doing this so intensely that she was exhausting herself mentally and emotionally. This, in turn, caused her to believe that her efforts had been as much physical as psychological. Suddenly, Melissa realized this, and her expression seemed to brighten. Her head lifted, her posture straightened, a smile came over her face, and she began to laugh.

"All these weeks. . . these past months I have been banging my head against a wall that doesn't even exist! How could doing so little feel so exhausting?" She smiled again and we all had a great laugh.

The change was immediate and startling. Within a few weeks her dating calendar was filling up, and she was having fun. She started attending singles events. She got in touch with some of the men she hadn't responded to online in her state of emotional exhaustion. She was finally making her search for love a reality by putting Action into the other Predictors. It didn't take long for her to find love, and when she did, she was able to embrace it.

In Melissa's story we can see how, even if all the other Predictors are in place, if the Action Predictor is not properly engaged, the other Predictors can't make a difference. Melissa really believed she was putting a lot of effort into dating, when in reality all of her effort was in her head. The Action Predictor was missing. Melissa thought she was taking actions and that they weren't producing results, which in turn threw off her emotional balance and began to erode her belief. It's as if she were sitting on a bicycle, thinking about pedaling furiously, but not actually touching her feet to the pedals, and not going anywhere. As soon as she realized this, her feet finally made contact with the pedals, and *zoom*, off she went! Again, it is important to note that even though the other five Predictors were working, the lack of one cancelled out the others.

More Is More

Another key component of the Action Predictor is taking *enough* action. We often see people taking too little action and deeming it enough. We have had clients come to us, choose to work with us, pay our fees, and then fail to adequately utilize our services. When we have introductions for them, they become difficult to reach. When they go on dates, they are slow to give us feedback and don't follow through with second dates that they themselves requested. We can only imagine that for these people, taking the initial steps is enough for them to believe that they are actively seeking love. You can go to a store and buy a spatula— a very nice spatula, top of the line— but this will not make you a gourmet cook. You have to take classes, and read books, and practice, and burn things, and throw them in the trash, and start all over again. Taking the initial step is a good start, but continuing to move forward, one action at a time, is essential to reaching any goal.

You have to get involved and stay involved. You, *yes*, you— the one who is reading these words right now! We're glad you picked up this book, and we're happy that you're reading it. Those were good actions, but simply buying and reading this book is not going to find you love. You need to take it further. You need to implement the advice we have shared, and put it into action. Think about how our stories relate to you. Think about which Predictors you are fully utilizing and which ones you need to work on. Think about how you are going to realize your dream— then put your plan into action!

The Comfort Zone

Staying inside your comfort zone feels good, but it is one of the most serious barriers to taking actions. Inside your comfort zone you will feel secure, comfortable and in control. Within its safe boundaries you don't have to take risks, or do anything new or difficult. As we go through life, we develop a number of typical responses to situations and experiences. In order to simplify decision-making, we create certain boundaries for ourselves. These boundaries are quick guides to what we consider safe areas— they minimize risk and ensure that consequences can be foreseen and effortlessly managed. Decisions based on this way of thinking can be as benign as always ordering the same meal at a restaurant because you know you like it and won't be disappointed, to as detrimental as turning down a wonderful job in another city for fear of all the changes the move will bring about.

If you are serious about finding love, you need to be willing to allow your search to take you places you would never have imagined yourself going. You have to allow your search to take you into situations that are unfamiliar and may make you uncomfortable. Of course we're not talking about dangerous places. However, if your search doesn't challenge you a little, then there's a good chance you are limiting your opportunities.

As we discussed in the chapter on the Open Predictor, risk is often precisely what is required. Finding love involves stretching yourself. You can think you are minimizing your risks by playing it safe and sticking to someone who conforms to your list of criteria. You can stay in your comfort zone by only looking for someone using a vehicle you are familiar with. In reality, you are only limiting your opportunities and likelihood of finding love. We would say that, more often than not, love exists outside your comfort zone. In order to find love, you need to break down some of the mental barriers that are keeping you locked into a life of either dating the wrong people, or simply staying single. And as we said before, it is not just a case of *thinking* about doing this, you have to actually *do* it. If you are confined to your comfort zone, you won't be taking the actions, or enough of the actions, that can make the difference.

We have a story which nicely portrays how staying in your comfort zone can keep you from taking action in your search for love. This story is about one of Susie's first clients, so we'll let her tell it. *Watch for how all of the other Predictors can't be effective without Action.*

Victoria – Beyond the Comfort Zone

One afternoon I had an appointment with a woman named Victoria. She was a high school vice-principal in her early 50s. When she arrived, we greeted each other and she sat down opposite me, scrutinizing me with a steely eye. As I began to speak, I felt an odd sensation creeping over me. I became flustered and tripped over my words. Taking a deep breath, I paused to gather myself. What was causing this feeling of nervousness? Then it hit me. This woman, who was seated across the desk from me, reminded me of the vice-principal I had when I was in high school— everything about her: from her hard gaze, to the way she sat with a straight back and her chin lifted as though she were looking down on me. It was the way she pursed her lips as I spoke, and the way one eyebrow wavered, as if she thought that what I was saying was nonsense. It was a strange experience. I, a grown woman, was shrinking. I was reverting to my 16-year-old self, trying to prove myself in a world of adults. A chill ran along my spine. I shook off these imaginings and concentrated on my job. This woman had come to me to find love, and I could help her.

She listened to what I had to say and answered my questions. After talking for a while and listening to Victoria explain the things she was willing to do to find love, I could see that Victoria had most of the Predictors in place. She talked about rearranging her schedule so that she would have more free evenings to go on dates, so I knew that she was making her search for love a priority. She said she believed that she was worthy of a loving partner and knew that, with time and effort, she would find the right person. When she described the kind of man she wanted to meet, her list was specific about his character and values rather than his physical attributes and background, so I was convinced she was open. When she told me about her dating history, I could see she understood that ups and downs were a natural part of the process, and that her emotional balance had always allowed her to handle them well.

As our conversation continued, she told me she wasn't use to discussing her personal life with other people. I noted that even with me, she hadn't been able to relax or develop a comfortable rapport. At the end of our conversation, she stood abruptly and said she wasn't sure this service was right for her and she wanted to go home to think about it. In my experience, when someone tells me they want to go home to think about something, it usually means they have already decided to discount my advice. Victoria told me she would call in a few days. I thanked her and said I would look forward to hearing from her, knowing full well that it was unlikely I would. I had the distinct impression she had taken a disliking to me.

I didn't hear from Victoria after a few days, nor after a few weeks. I assumed that she did indeed dislike me, and that her dislike was standing in the way of her moving forward with our service. Perhaps she really did want to find love, just not with my help. I wondered why I wasn't able to connect with her. Had I been cold towards her? Was it the flashback to my high school years that had tainted our relationship so quickly? I felt disappointed for her. Victoria did have four of the Predictors in place. She knew what it would take to find love, the necessity of making her search a priority, being open, emotionally balanced, and having positive belief. What was left was for her to take action and find an effective vehicle to get her there. However, that would mean taking a step out of her comfort zone.

Perhaps the problem wasn't me at all. Maybe it was knowing that she would have to leave the safety of her comfort zone that had frightened her away. Victoria was a private person and asking for help in such a personal area of her life was not something she had ever done or ever wanted to do. By choosing my service as her vehicle, she would be taking an action that would invite me into her personal life. If she worked with me, I would be helping her with many important aspects of her dating life— from talking with her about her potential dates, to discussing how the date went, and even giving her feedback from the men she met. And then there was the fact that she would be going on dates and sharing details about her life with more new people. In my experience, for particularly private people, taking an action that opens their lives up to new people can be daunting. But engaging with my own sense of emotional balance and perspective, I had to accept the situation for what it was and let go of my disappointment.

About two months later, we had a special offer on sign-up fees. I was going through my list of callbacks when I came-across Victoria's name. I decided I would give her a call and see if she might be interested in trying again.

"Hi, Victoria. This is Susie, the matchmaker. Listen, I was just calling to tell you about this great offer we have at the moment. . . I was thinking that maybe you might want to make a decision and start moving your life in the direction of love?"

CLICK.

She hung up on me.

"Really? Did that just happen?" I remember sitting there at my desk, with the phone still pressed against my ear, in a minor state of shock. I was not used to being hung up on. Those people who really did not want to work with me usually made excuses, apologized, and then politely ended the phone call. This was something else. I put the phone down and stared at it for about a minute, my heart pounding. This was some kind of provocation.

It could have been the shock of what had just happened, or it could have been some kind of teenage authority-challenging flashback. But whatever it was, I was feeling feisty and my mind was made up. I picked up the phone and dialed Victoria's number again. When she answered, I spoke quickly.

"Victoria? You can hang up on me all you want, but you know what? You're alone, and if you want that to change, you have to do something about it."

There was a long silence on the other end of the line. For a moment I thought she had already hung up on me again. Then I noticed the low murmur of a radio or television coming from her end. It sounded so very distant, but I knew Victoria was still there, still weighing my words, still thinking about what she wanted for her life. At last I heard a deep sigh. Then she spoke.

"You're right," she said. In that preceding silence, I believe she realized that, in the two months since she had been in my office, nothing in her love life had changed. Taking on a vehicle might not be easy, but she knew it was time to push herself to take action, even if it meant being uncomfortable.

She came in the next day, and we went over the matchmaking process again. I explained that we would work with her to choose the kind of people she would enjoy meeting, and when I had an introduction for her, I would call her and tell her about him. I would work with her to set up a date where they could meet and comfortably get to know each other. I promised her that she could set her own pace for dating. I reminded her that the people we would introduce her to were looking for the same thing she was; someone wonderful who they could share their life with. She had questions— lots of questions. I answered them all. At last, she took a breath, and told me she was ready to take action and move her life forward.

Throughout all the time I worked with Victoria, I never really shook off the silly high school vibe, and, I imagine, she never let go of her opinion of me as a pushy woman who wouldn't take maybe for an answer. Still, together we went about changing her life.

My initial observation that Victoria had the Predictors in place was correct. All of them except Vehicle and Action, and those two were kick-started by my insistence. Eight months later, Victoria was engaged. Having fallen in love with a wonderful man, all Victoria's exterior coldness had gone; her defenses had been lowered. The day she came into the office to show off her engagement ring, she was all smiles. No longer the stern vice-principal, she seemed more like a giddy teenager. What a turnaround! I, beaming like a vindicated vice-principal at a graduation ceremony, wished her well as she started down a new road on the journey of life.

Two people had to exit their comfort zones for Victoria's life to change. Susie exited her comfort zone when she chose to take a risk and challenge Victoria's closed-off response to the follow-up call. Victoria left hers behind when she moved out of inertia into action. Thinking she knew what was involved in the search for love, she took an initial action by contacting us. However, when Victoria realized she would have to open up to new people and let Susie help her, she retreated with the excuse that she needed to think about it. Then, when Susie decided to call her months later, her reaction was to cut off the conversation. Click. Call ended, problem gone. Had she not allowed herself to be swayed by Susie's determination, she would have stayed in her comfort zone and never met the love of her life.

Maintaining Momentum

The last bit of wisdom we can take from Victoria's story is to strike while the iron is hot. Take action when the emotional upheaval is immediate. When someone turns to us, it is because they have been pushed into action by some internal or external motivator. If time passes, or something else happens, they will get distracted and the urgency will dissipate. The iron grows cold and the action fizzles out. Victoria might have gone home and begun thinking about working with Susie to find love. However, she never made a decision. Whatever had spurred her to meet with Susie in the first place was forgotten and life just went back to normal. As Cinderella from *Into the Woods* said so wisely, "Opportunity is not a lengthy visitor."

You also need a steady, consistent expenditure of energy. If you know what drove you to the point of action, it is essential that you hold onto it. Remember the feeling that was so strong that it ignited your desire to change your life. Write it down, so that in a few days or weeks, when the iron cools, you can recall what it was that inspired you. It is up to you to keep the Action Predictor going— to energize all of the other Predictors and keep yourself on the road to love. Again, let's use the analogy of riding a bike. You need to give yourself a good push to get started. Now imagine you are riding on a flat country road. The preliminary push will pretty soon peter out and you will come to a stop. In order to keep yourself moving forward, you need to apply continuous energy. If you pedal too hard, you may go fast, but you will needlessly exhaust yourself and may not make it to the finish. Not pedaling enough will result in an irregular stop and start motion that will not get you to where you are going very quickly or comfortably. Action needs to be steady and consistent.

Then, consider the fact that the road to love is *not* a continuously flat surface. The dating experience has an irregular terrain; it is made up of hopeful beginnings and sad endings, exciting moments and anxious uncertainties. Sustaining Action's momentum is an integral part of maintaining Balance throughout the journey. In order to enjoy the ease and fun of a good date, or the exciting early days of a relationship, you will have to face some trials: first dates, nerves, and disappointments. When the the road ahead looks like a long uphill climb, it is easy to justify stopping to rest. Momentum is what will keep you going and get you to the finish. Good momentum can only be achieved with a consistent and well-paced expenditure of your energy.

Avoid Spinning Your Wheels

Let's make sure all of your effort makes an impact. Even if you are consistently putting your desires into action, if the other Predictors are not applied, no amount of action will prevail. You will take action after action, doing and more doing, but you will just be spinning your wheels. You will be working much harder than you should with nothing to show for it. As you fire all your engines, remember to keep the other Predictors in mind— just like a pilot checks his instruments before takeoff.

Now let's examine a case that demonstrates why the Action Predictor is not enough on its own. This story goes back to before Susie and Elizabeth started working together as matchmakers, so we'll let Elizabeth begin. . . *Watch for how Action can't be effective without all of the other Predictors.*

Sydney – The Saboteur

Before I met Susie, I worked as a Dating and Relationship Coach. Sydney was my very first paying client. She was a tall, striking brunette in her mid-thirties, and she had come to me to help her find love, marriage, and the chance of starting a family. She worked as a nanny and adored kids, so it was only right that she should have her own. Sydney had a great attitude and no trouble getting dates. She'd had a few relationships— some good and some not so good. The problem, as far as she saw it, was that when she was in a relationship that she felt was working well, she was unable to keep it going. It always ended. No matter what she tried, she couldn't make it stick. This pattern was beginning to take its toll on her naturally sunny disposition.

We worked well together. We identified the areas in her life she needed to change and came up with strategies to implement those changes. Yet, it seemed that whenever I gave her solid, dependable advice, she would ignore it and do the opposite. If I said, "Don't call that guy, give it a little time," she would go home and make the call. If I said not to mention the priority of having children on a first date, Sydney would do precisely that. It was a strange situation. She listened to what I said, she agreed, she took notes, and then she didn't follow my advice. She was, for all intents and purposes, the saboteur of her own love life.

Later, when I met Susie and we began our matchmaking partnership, Sydney expressed an interest in what we were doing. She got involved, helping set up events, and attending our classes. When the business began to grow, Sydney came to work for us part-time. She enjoyed helping our clients and was always thinking of them. All the while, she was doing everything she could to find love: she had joined a social group for meeting men, she let her friends fix her up, and she used online dating services. All the same, she was still failing. As she watched the women we matched find love and happiness, she wondered about her own inability to find love.

There was no doubt that her Action Predictor was in place. She continued to search for a life partner and spread her efforts across a number of vehicles. As for Priority, it could not be faulted. She changed her career to make herself more available for finding love. Maybe because she always knew there would be more men to date, or maybe because she had two matchmakers looking out for her, she kept her perspective through the ups and downs. Sydney had the Balance Predictor.

As time passed, Sydney kept a close eye on which of our clients were successful, and she began to notice a couple of important factors. More often than not, those people who were truly open were the ones who found love. She assessed her own criteria and, realizing how restrictive it had been, she decided to take action to widen her search. She allowed herself to be open to possibilities she would have previously dismissed. In the past, she only wanted to date men who were older than herself. Realizing that she was really looking for someone who was mature and shared her life goals, she opened her search to men who were within ten years of her own age. Previously, she had limited herself to dating men who were 6'2" or above. Now, she was open to dating men who were her height or taller. These adjustments in her criteria increased her available candidates by thousands of men.

Sydney also saw that those people who believed they could find love usually did. She questioned her own belief, and discussed it with us. With a bit more time, she was able to understand that, despite her determination and the amount of action she was taking, there remained a little voice in the back of her head that warned her not to be too optimistic. It was a subtle note of caution that caused her to avoid being fully committed. It was the voice that whispered, late at night, "Don't get your hopes up— you'll only get hurt."

With our help and her natural determination, Sydney began to turn her disempowering belief around. She found the courage to take action to address that voice when it began to whisper. She forced it to the front of her mind where she could confront it. She reminded herself that the little voice was not the truth, but just her fears of being disappointed and hurt again. She told herself that, while being hurt was always a risk, she trusted herself to make good choices. She assured herself that she would be OK if things didn't work out. This process allowed Sydney to turn her disempowering belief back into a doubt or fear that she could experience and then let go— making room for the empowering belief that she, like the clients she was helping, could have love in her life.

Soon after she began to work on her openness and belief, I happened to have my bedroom remodeled. The man doing the work was very friendly and easy-going. I remember standing in the doorway to the bedroom as he worked and asking him if he was single. He immediately became uncomfortable. I was blocking his only exit and asking him about his love life. He discreetly lowered his voice.

"Excuse me, but I do believe you are a married woman," he carefully reminded me.

That day I learned to explain my job before asking such a personal question! I told him all about my work, and he lightened up again. "Yeah, I'm single. Why? You think you can help me meet a nice woman?"

I ran off and got a photo of Sydney. There was something about this guy that made me think of her. It was just a feeling; an intuition. I showed him the photo. He couldn't help the smile that spread over his face. He told me he thought she was beautiful and asked if she was as nice as she looked. "Even more so," I answered confidently. I knew that Sydney would be working at our next event and I told him he had to come. He said he would. Not good enough. I got him to take out his calendar and made him mark the date then and there. He laughed and did so.

He came to the event and met Sydney. He was, as he said himself, "blown away." For him, it was love at first sight. Nervously, he asked her out, and Sydney accepted. For Sydney, accepting the invitation was a big step, since he didn't perfectly match all of the criteria she considered important for a future husband. He wasn't 6'2". He was two years younger than her. He didn't like football. (She was a huge college football fan and, as a season ticket holder at her alma mater, she wanted to be with someone who would love going to the games with her.) He loved steak and had always prided himself on his barbecue skills, while she was an animal lover and had always been a vegetarian. Despite the fact that she would have once thought they were a mismatch, she allowed herself to explore the connection.

They dated and eventually began a relationship. Having finally disarmed that little voice, Sydney allowed herself to fall completely in love with him, too. She told us that he was more wonderful than any man she had ever dreamed of. They had a beautiful wedding and now share a wonderful life. He had a son from a previous marriage and Sydney is now a happy and loving stepmother.

When it came to the Action Predictor, Sydney was putting in the effort, and her dedication to making it happen was nothing less than impressive. But, as we can see, without the Open and Belief Predictors, Sydney was going in circles and wasting all the energy she was putting into Action.

Taking Action

There will be times when you won't feel like working with your vehicle or going on another date, and times when you have become disillusioned, or even angry, with the process. This is when action keeps you in the game. The first and most powerful action you can take is to make sure all of the other Predictors are in place. Make love your *priority* and anchor your *belief* that you can attain love. Be fully *open* to finding love, achieve emotional *balance,* and choose the best *vehicles* for you. Then you will find that *action* is already well on the way to becoming a reality. Just remember this: action is what happens in the world. **Wishing it to happen is not the same as making it happen.**

If you find yourself thinking, "I'm in action all the time, but I'm not getting the results I want," you need to look at the other Predictors and find out why your actions are not successful. That said, it is not just a question of having five Predictors in place and assuming Action will take care of itself. Action, as the word itself suggests, demands physical effort. It requires animation, movement, and the physical expression of energy. You need to walk your talk. Take the actions that express what you want your life to be. And when you do begin to take action, make sure it is coming from the right place— an uplifting and empowering belief.

Be consistent in your actions and in your efforts for dating. You need to plan your actions, and make sure you follow through. Get a coach, a dating buddy, or a friend who shares your goals to keep you accountable. Tell them about your plans for finding a partner, and ask them to hold you to your commitment of taking actions. Keep a journal that chronicles your actions. This way, you will be able to see what you are and aren't doing. It will help you to stay organized. Above all, give yourself credit for your hard work!

You've thought long and hard about finding love. You've established that you want love and it is your *priority*. You have positive *belief*, are *open* in your search for love, have emotional *balance* and have chosen the *vehicles* to find your life partner. It's time to go beyond the thinking and get into *action*. Know that the actions you take— and take *consistently*— will make the difference.

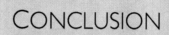

CONCLUSION

CONCLUSION

THE INSIGHTS we have shared with you are the culmination of our decades of experience working as matchmakers. We've had years of trial and error and years of refining our working process. We have worked with thousands of singles, made a multitude of matches, witnessed a fair few heartbreaks and countless happy couples. We've pretty much seen it all. This wealth of first-hand knowledge allowed us to discover, explore, and fine-tune The Six Predictors. It has been extremely rewarding to help our clients apply The Six Predictors to their dating processes and to witness the empowering difference The Predictors have made.

Now, here's the cool thing— you've read this book, and now you too have the Matchmaker Secrets for dating success. With this information, you have the power to take control of your dating life and your search for love. You can leave behind the days of waiting for Cupid to choose you as his next target. You can give up the notion that love is only for the lucky, and know that you are the driver of your destiny.

Use The Six Predictors the way we do with our clients. Each person we work with comes to us with the desire to make a change in their dating life. We use the Six Predictors to help them see their strengths and identify where they are faltering in their search. We give them The Six Predictors as a guidance system. Like a dating GPS, the Predictors tell them where they are and how to reach their destination. So, when you feel that your dating life isn't working for you, look to The Six Predictors. When you feel that you are lost in your search for love, look to The Six Predictors. When you are dating regularly, but still can't seem to develop the connections you have made, look to The Six Predictors. If you are exhausting yourself, with nothing to show for it, look to The Six Predictors. Whenever you feel restricted, inhibited, or discouraged, look to The Predictors. Use them to guide you.

The Priority Predictor – Give yourself permission to make your search for love a central part of your life. Let your search take precedence, and give it the attention it deserves.

The Belief Predictor – Know that love is attainable for you. Nurture your inner truth. Know that a person who is right for you exists and that you will have the ability to find them.

The Open Predictor – Remember that love is looking for you, so be open to how it shows up. Free yourself from the constraints of your preconceived ideals and allow love to surprise you.

The Balance Predictor – Protect yourself from the extreme highs and lows of dating. Foster and maintain emotional balance by keeping your perspective as you navigate the delights and disappointments throughout the process.

The Vehicle Predictor – Give love a way to find you and give yourself a way to find love. To reach your destination, you need a means of getting there. Make use of a variety of vehicles for meeting other great single people.

The Action Predictor – Take action— find love. Move yourself from thinking about finding love to actually *doing* it. Bring Action to all of the other predictors, and bring the other Predictors to Action, so that your search can reach its full potential.

Remember that the Predictors all work together and rely on each other.

As you go through the dating process, regularly check in with each Predictor. Doing so can be a wonderful tool to help you stay on track. In particular, make sure to check your progress with the Predictors that you know you need to work on. Always allow yourself the time to see results.

Now that you know The Six Predictors and are using them regularly, you can go through the dating process with a little less weight on your shoulders. You no longer have the stress of wondering if you should make love a *priority.* You've made the decision, and now you can move on. You have the peace of mind that comes with your *belief* that you will find love. You no longer have the pressure to find the "perfect match" because you are *open* to letting love surprise you. You can be confident that your emotional *balance* will keep the ups and downs of dating from interfering with your search. You know that, with your chosen *vehicles,* you have many ways and many opportunities to find love. And best of all, you can be confident that you are taking *actions* that support your goal.

Keep these points in mind, and you can avoid the frustrations and pitfalls of the dating world. But above all, make sure you *enjoy* the process. Remember, dating is about having fun. Lighten the load of pressure you put on yourself and on the people you meet, and the weight of expectation will be reduced. See every date you go on as an opportunity to learn something, to make a new friend, and to have fun.

While we have written this book as a guide to finding love, the Six Predictors can be used as a roadmap to realizing any goal. Looking for a new job? Well, you're going to need to make it a *priority*. You will need the *belief* you can get a job. You need to be *open* to new kinds of work. Maintaining *balance* is essential to handle anticipation and disappointments. A *vehicle* for seeking out the available jobs is indispensable. Finally, you need *action* to get yourself out there and engage in your search. Take these Six Predictors to heart, and you will find that you can apply them to a vast array of life challenges. Quit smoking, lose weight, find a new house, pass a class— you name it. The Six Predictors will adapt themselves to all of these goals and more. And even if, when all is said and done, you find that you want a little more joy in your life, apply The Six Predictors and start making it a reality. The Predictors give you the power to be successful in all areas of life and, most importantly, in finding love.

You now have the inside scoop. You don't have to find these answers through endless trial and error. We have put in the years of matching, watching, learning, noting the failures, and celebrating the successes, to discover the Predictors. They are signposts to your goal, but they are also much more than that. The Six Predictors are a challenge, a roadmap, a blueprint for a better life, and it is *you* who must implement them. You have control over these Predictors. With their guidance, you can shift your thoughts and behaviors, you can change your approach to dating, and you can empower yourself to find love.

Contrary to much of the conventional wisdom, you have a great deal of influence in how your love life will unfold. You have the power to be successful. We have faith in you. Now, get out there, have some fun, and find the love you are looking for!

A Gift from the Matchmakers!

Now that you have read our book and learned our secrets, we would like to give you a special gift to help you use the Six Predictors in your search for love.

Your gift is waiting for you at:

http://MatchmakerSecrets.com/gift

Enter this code: Secret6P

If you'd like more information about…

- Professional Matchmaking Services
- Online Profile Makeovers
- Online Dating Coaching
- Dating and Relationship Coaching
- Image Consulting
- The MS. Club— an Exclusive Social Club for Single Women
- Education: Classes, Workshops, and Webinars
- How to arrange for Elizabeth and Susie to speak to your organization, group, or book club

…Contact us at
info@MatchmakerSecrets.com
or visit www.MatchmakerSecrets.com

ABOUT THE AUTHORS

Elizabeth Cobey-Piper and Susie Hardesty are both dedicated and passionate professional matchmakers certified through the Matchmaking Institute in New York City. Together, they have over 30 years of experience helping singles reach their goals of finding love and fulfilling relationships! Through their results driven approach to matchmaking and close partnerships with their clients, these devoted matchmakers help the people they work with open their hearts and enjoy the journey.

Elizabeth took a circuitous route to her matchmaking career. In 2004, after more than 20 years of working with museums, galleries, universities, and state institutions to accomplish multi-million dollar objectives, Elizabeth decided to take her exceptional marketing and motivational experience and focus on her passion for helping individuals. The result was her unique dating and relationship coaching program that helped her clients to uncover their obstacles, discover their true potential, and learn to communicate the best versions of themselves.

Susie began her career as a professional matchmaker in 1992. After 10 successful years as the director of a high-end dating service where she matched many happy couples, Susie struck out on her own to realize her cherished dream of founding a matchmaking company. Susie's amazing insight and incredible methods for successful dating are the result of her years of experience, innate enthusiasm, inexhaustible persistence, and her extraordinary vision.

Elizabeth and Susie's business partnership began in 2005 when they combined Susie's thriving matchmaking and singles events company with Elizabeth's dating and relationship coaching practice. Together they envisioned a matchmaking service that would make a bigger difference in people's lives. Their goal was to design a multidimensional approach to matchmaking that would empower their clients, increase their confidence, introduce them to amazing people, and stack the odds of finding love in their favor. Their merger was a success! To date, their companies, Matchmaker Secrets, Dating Directions, and Affinity Matchmaking, have helped thousands of singles succeed in their dating lives and ultimately find healthy and passionate relationships.

Elizabeth and Susie say that matchmaking is hard work 90% of the time, and 10% of the experience is glamorous and fun. But overall, it's 100% worth it. For them, the most rewarding aspect of their work is seeing the happiness of the people they have matched; they love attending weddings and seeing photos of dream vacations and new babies.

Elizabeth Cobey-Piper   Susie Hardesty